'Because [Zábrana] was primarily interested in authors who had been persecuted—such as Babel, Mandelstam, Bunin and Solzhenitsyn—he was very thorough when it came to obtaining information about them that "was very often not widely available, such as the executions of Babel and Mandelstam, which were hushed up for a long time". For this reason, Aleš Kisil [a Czech film-maker who made a documentary about Zábrana's life] maintains that Zábrana did his utmost to find "credible and objective sources" of information in the USSR. "It's possible—and actually even probable—that he could have met someone from this circle of people who told him about the assassination of Camus, and who themselves had heard it from someone close to the upper echelons of the Communist Party at that time," Kisil said.'

—*Radio Free Europe/Radio Liberty*

'*The Death of Camus* contends that the KGB was responsible for the auto accident that killed Camus [...] Perhaps even more controversially, Catelli also argues that the French government was complicit in the killing, with some in the intelligence community believing it necessary in order to improve relations between the two countries.'

—*Inside Hook*

'Catelli learned not to give up hope in all the time that has passed since he discovered the testimony of Jan Zábrana. His book reads like a detective novel without resolution or punishment—no one was or will be jailed for having murdered Camus —but with a compensatory narrative justice.'

—*Pagina 12* (Argentina)

'A text of seductive literary, biographical, critical and histo⌐⌐ value.'

'Catelli succeeds in convincing us that Camus could have been assassinated by the KGB.'

—*Le Monde Libertaire*

'Fast-paced and entertaining, *The Death of Camus* reads like a spy novel.'

—*La Capital* (Argentina)

THE DEATH OF CAMUS

GIOVANNI CATELLI

The Death of Camus

Translated by
Andrew Tanzi

HURST & COMPANY, LONDON

First published in Italian in 2013 as *Camus deve morire*
© 2013 Nutrimenti srl.
Via Marco Aurelio 44—00184 Rome, Italy

This translation first published in the United Kingdom in 2020 by
C. Hurst & Co. (Publishers) Ltd.,
41 Great Russell Street, London, WC1B 3PL
English translation © Andrew Tanzi, 2020
Foreword © Paul Auster, 2020
All rights reserved.
Printed in Great Britain by Bell and Bain Ltd, Glasgow

A Cataloguing-in-Publication data record for this book
is available from the British Library.

ISBN: 9781787383869

This book is printed using paper from registered sustainable
and managed sources.

www.hurstpublishers.com

In memory of Imre Nagy and Salvador Allende

Wreckage from the car crash in which Camus died.

CONTENTS

CONTENTS

"Wrongs that are not righted within a generation simply vanish—it's as if nothing ever happened. Everything disappears—the killers and the killed."

Jan Zábrana

LIST OF PHOTOGRAPHS

Wreckage from the car crash in which Camus died.
(Keystone-France\Gamma-Rapho via Getty Images)

Rescuers take a last look at the shattered wreck of the custom built Facel Vega car in which Albert Camus and Michel Gallimard were travelling.
Bettman/Getty Images.

Albert Camus's coffin being carried from Villeblevin Town Hall on the way to internment at Lourmarin in the Vaucluse, 5 January 1960.
Keystone-France\Gamma-Rapho (via Getty Images)

Albert Camus receives the Nobel Prize for literature; applauding him, Queen Louise Mountbatten and King Gustav VI Adolf of Sweden, Stockholm (Sweden), 10 December 1957
Farabola/Alamy Stock Photo

Albert Camus signing copies of *The Rebel* with a wrapper announcing he had won the Nobel Prize for Literature
INTERFOTO/Alamy Stock Photo

Imre Nagy, Prime Minister of Premier of Hungary during the 1956 Revolt against the Soviets. Nagy was

executed for treason in 1958, an event that greatly angered Camus.
Everett Collection Historical/Alamy Stock Photo

Dmitri Shepilov, former Minister of Foreign Affairs of the Soviet Union, photographed in 1955
The Dutch National Archives, via Creative Commons Attribution-Share Alike 3.0 Netherlands license.

Albert Camus (1913–1960)
Granger Historical Picture Archive/Alamy Stock Photo

Boris Leonidovich Pasternak, 1890-1960, Russian novelist and admirer of Camus
INTERFOTO/Alamy Stock Photo

Albert Camus
Granger Historical Picture Archive/Alamy Stock Photo

Plaques in Villeblevin commemorating the death of Camus
Photos courtesy and © Dr Tony Shaw

ACKNOWLEDGEMENTS

The author wishes to thank Marie Zábranová for her support and encouragement, as well as for the documentation provided. He also wishes to thank Herbert Lottman and Marianne Véron Lottman for their friendship, help and precious recollections.

FOREWORD

Paul Auster

In this disturbing book, Giovanni Catelli sets out to solve the riddle of the car accident that killed Albert Camus and his publisher, Michel Gallimard, on 4 January, 1960. Based on years of meticulous research, the author builds a compelling argument to support his contention that they were the victims of premeditated murder. A horrible conclusion, but after digesting the evidence Catelli has given us, it becomes difficult not to agree with him. Thus "car accident" should now be filed in another drawer as "political assassination"—and thus Albert Camus was silenced when he was forty-six years old.

INTRODUCTION

Albert Camus was a free, indomitable and dangerous man.

He was a threat to all the powers that be, promptly denouncing any abuse, brutality or injustice they committed.

His critical spirit, his inflexible honesty, as well as his unconditional love for mankind and for life enabled him to see beyond the surface of things. He was a threat to those with a dirty conscience among the French and the Algerian rebels, the old collaborationists and Stalinists, the middle-class moralists and high society.

His death—and thus his silencing for good—benefitted many: the French Nationalists, who were resisting the campaign for an independent Algeria; the Algerian extremists, who recoiled at his moderate stance on the fate of the *pieds-noirs*—French Algerians—in the event of Algerian independence; the reactionary forces, who saw him as a champion of the Resistance and the left wing; the Stalinists and the Soviet Union, whom he had bitterly criticised following their brutal attack on Hungary; General Franco's fascist dictatorship, which he opposed in his public speeches, seizing every chance to denounce it so that Western countries would deny Spain a place in the international community of nations.

It has always been hard to believe that Camus died as the result of a commonplace car accident. Fate doesn't conspire against a man just like that—that's something men do. And now a crystal-clear clue has emerged from the indistinct flow of time, suggesting a name, an order, a will to kill. Yes, perhaps someone really did decide Albert Camus had to die. Having found that clue, it is our duty to dig deeper so that past events may not be forgotten. Instead, let us ensure that the light of the present, the light of historical investigation shines at last on the naked truth of certain events and, ultimately, let us make it known and understood to future generations.

During our investigation we shall meet real, living protagonists—all characters of great literary and human depth whose paths crossed with Camus' often in an unpredictable but always fruitful and sometimes decisive manner.

These protagonists lived in Prague and Moscow. Their names are Jan Zábrana, Marie Zábranová and Boris Pasternak. Prague and Moscow—as well as Paris, of course—can tell us the truth about Albert Camus' fate.

A CONSPIRACY

Albert Camus died on 4 January 1960. The man who spent his life fighting to defend others from injustice and absurdity perished for no discernible reason. And the apparent cause of his death was what he himself had dubbed the pinnacle of absurdity: a car crash.

Camus was heading to Paris. His publisher and friend Michel Gallimard was at the wheel. They had just had lunch and were cruising along a wide, straight road in broad daylight. Nothing boded ill.

Then, all of a sudden, tragedy struck. Passing motorists said the speeding car was "waltzing". It skidded left and right with such violence that the back-seat passengers (the publisher's wife and daughter) thought Gallimard was trying to negotiate an unexpected bend. It was as if "something was crumbling underneath them". Then the car smashed into one of the trees lining the road, ricocheted against another a few metres further on and was completely destroyed. His skull split open and neck broken, Albert Camus died on the spot.

Michel Gallimard was found on the ground in a pool of his own blood; he would die in hospital a few days later. His wife was next to him in a state of shock; their daughter had landed in a field some twenty metres away, dazed but miraculously unhurt.

According to his biographer, the late Herbert R. Lottman, "The accident seemed to have been caused by a blowout or a broken axle; experts were puzzled by it happening on a long stretch of straight road, a road 30 feet wide, and with little traffic at the time."

There you have it.

Right from the outset, the events that occurred and their logical explanation did not match up. One has to wonder whether the mundane outward signs were not concealing the truth—a design, perhaps, hidden behind something so trivial.

Many refused to believe that the accident and Camus' death were the mere work of fate; it was all too obvious. Something didn't quite fit; surely it was far too ironic that destiny had lined up so flawlessly with Camus' almost supernatural omen.

None of those who loved Camus and cherished his dignity and his teachings could find a shred of credibility in the facile evidence; how could fate and foreboding have lined up so perfectly? Years later, other silent followers would also find that trivial accident inadequate, inauthentic, almost a poor and gratuitous *coup de theatre*.

An unspoken certainty haunted them for ages, as would a lingering restlessness, a feeling of having been deceived and the impression that some hidden machination had taken place.

But then, one day, a clue in the form of an unexpected account came out of the blue. It was the undying proof that had stood the test of time—the vital clue that turned external appearances on their head and revealed a conspiracy.

SYMMETRY

Fate is a wonderful thing. In an instant it can make age-old problems, inextricable issues and awkward cases come to a head.

One day, a world-renowned intellectual—whose commitment was manifest on several fronts and who stood alone against the strongest powers of the day—said that the pinnacle of absurdity would be to die in a car crash. And that was just how he died, as if to reveal some absurd machination.

The illusory symmetry of fate had come full circle, clinching fate's master plan and indulging an involuntary prophecy; Camus' omen had been proven spot on.

A massive deception was fed to everyone, no matter how sensible or oblivious they were, irrespective of whether they were intellectuals rather than members of the general public, or even haters rather than followers. Symmetry lay in the ambush, in the threat and in the inexplicable consequence—an outcome just as absurd and flawless as it was designed to be. What better fate could befall the extreme consistency, the prophecy come true, the end that confirmed the lucid purpose of a life?

What better blend of truth and deception, absurdity and conspiracy, fate and design, prophecy and execution could there be?

Reality and hard facts could not survive such perfection, such a flawless convergence of fate and machination, the absolute accident and the absolute sabotage rolled into one. Fifty years later we are still trapped in this mortal embrace of truth and illusion, where the evidence seems to cancel out even the mere thought of an ambush.

And yet, fate hadn't quite buried those events for good; in fact, over the years it spread traces of the truth. The most obvious were left in Prague in 1980, twenty years after the crash. These traces are decisive; they are stone cold in their precision and thoroughness, so detailed and connected to unquestionable facts and dates that nobody could know of them in Czechoslovakia in 1980, when the country was in the Soviet stranglehold that had been growing tighter and tighter since the emergence of the Charter 77 dissident movement. Fate handed these traces to a defeated man who had resigned himself to the overwhelming righteousness of history, to personal downfall, to the lucidity of his despair. This individual preserved them without ever mentioning them to anyone.

He died a few years later.

This man was a poet, a translator and a silent, implacable witness to the misery that history bestowed on his country, his parents and even him. He knew he would have to succumb but not without remembering, not without writing a memory of the decay, a chronology of a collapse.

We do not know whether he did it for himself or for those who would, one day, pore over the memories of those years. We also know that he kept a diary, filling it with events and thoughts in his daily fight against disgust and humiliation.

He resisted for years.

Then he fell ill.

He entrusted his papers to his beloved wife. He died.

He was the Prague man.

THE DREAM

On the night of 2 January, 1960, Albert had a long, disturbing nightmare.

The sun was setting; Camus was being pursued along a country road by four faceless men. They seemed to be holding back, as if they didn't really want to catch up with him. Still, they inched closer and closer, more and more menacingly.

Camus ran on, despite his weak lungs. Gasping for air, he turned now and then to make sure he was still at a safe distance. He tried to identify those rubber faces in spite of their smooth, featureless outlines.

He ran for what seemed like forever, with no thoughts other than escaping, desperately gulping down the air and sounding like a drowning man. Suddenly, he saw a car coming from a side road. He stopped at the crossroads and started waving his arms; the car stopped, he jumped in and the car skidded off.

He tried to catch his breath. He tried to make out the driver's face but it was shrouded in complete darkness.

The car went faster and faster, tearing through the deserted, unknown and featureless countryside.

Camus asked the driver a question but got no answer. The silence in the passenger compartment grew heavier and heavier. Suddenly, the headlights lit up a broad bend and the high wall of a country house straight ahead. The car shot forward; the driver didn't even try to swerve.

Just when the crash seemed inevitable, Camus cried out and flung himself on the wheel. Right then, he fell out of bed and woke up, gasping in anguish.

THE JOURNEY

Even though he had purchased a train ticket to travel with René Char, on 3 January Camus got into the car of his friend and publisher Michel Gallimard and left his house in Lourmarin, in the south of France. He was heading to Paris. With them were Gallimard's wife Anne and daughter Janine, as well as their dog. Since there was no more room in the car, Char would take the train as planned.

The day before, Camus had dropped his wife Francine and their children at the railway station in Avignon, so they could head straight home.

On the morning of the 3rd he called his secretary in Paris to tell her which assignments to decline and to confirm he was on his way back.

Maybe the call was intercepted; in any case, several sources could have reported precisely on Camus' next movements.

On 30 December he had written to the actress Catherine Sellers, one of his lovers, to tell her he would be back soon. He wrote to her again the next day, opening with "This is my last letter..." and saying exactly when he would be back: "See you on Tuesday, my love. I'm dying to kiss you…"

On the 30th he had also written to the most important woman in his life, his long-time partner, the actress María Casares, detailing his plans. "This is my last letter… just to let you know I'll be back on Tuesday. I'm coming back by car with the Gallimards on Monday. (They're dropping by on Friday. I'll call you when I get home but we can plan to have dinner together on Tuesday)."

Several people could have been privy to Camus' plans and movements with sufficient notice. The two actresses' entourages were rife with characters who might leak such news: Casares was acquainted with several politically engaged individuals and the news she received was more accurate; perhaps she unwittingly provided the killers with crucial information.

On 29 December Camus had also written to Mi, a new partner of his in Denmark, telling her he would soon be heading back to Paris.

Many people had access to Camus' plans and would have known of his intention to return by car to Paris with the Gallimards.

There was plenty of time to set up an operation. It was a huge opportunity.

THE DEPARTURE

So on the morning of 3 January Camus, as was his custom, gave the house keys to Mme Ginoux, telling her he'd be back in eight days at the most. He got into Gallimard's powerful Facel Vega HK500 and they headed off.

A few days earlier, the publisher Robert Laffont had suggested that Michel Gallimard should take a train to the south of France; Gallimard, however, insisted he wanted to visit Camus and travel with him on the way back.

Fate's machinations are often evanescent, random and fleeting, suddenly coalescing as if by magic; on other occasions they leave an indelible mark, converging from afar with a meticulously planned design.

On that day, the car and those men had their paths marked out for them. And other men would follow the same path.

After bidding farewell to their friends Mathieu and Jacques Polge, the group set off along Route Nationale 7 to Orange, where they stopped for lunch.

A fast driver by nature, that day Michel Gallimard decided to take it easy and chat with his family and friend as they cruised along.

That may be what saved the passengers' lives—at least for the time being. But someone was travelling with them, silently, in the shadows.

There was still plenty of road to cover and with it came many opportunities to act.

In the afternoon the four set off again, heading for the hotel restaurant Le Chapon Fin, in the village of Thoissey just outside Mâcon. They had booked a few rooms there so they could break the journey and avoid getting caught up in the heavy inbound traffic of holidaymakers heading home. They weren't in a hurry. And fate had its plans laid out.

The overnight stay would provide some relief from the long journey; the next day they would head to Paris, rested, unhurried.

It would be a long night at the village. Not everyone would sleep. The travellers were merry and didn't know any better.

A lavish dinner and a friendly atmosphere awaited them. Everything seemed to bode well. The secret laws of repression seemed light-years away.

The crushing grip of the powers that be on the fate of the individual were invisible, remote and even unreal.

So let us leave these men and women to their final hours of happiness.

THE PRAGUE MAN

The Prague man was a poet. History had already taken its toll on him through his loved ones. His socialist parents had been persecuted and imprisoned by the regime after 1948. He had witnessed them wither and die under the weight of imprisonment, deprivation and illness. A whole generation's hope for a fairer society had soon been crushed by bureaucracy, by obtuse oppression and by the secret police.

Literature was his refuge from life's never-ending adversities, daily hardships and the progressive dissolution of hope and delusion. The art of translation and poetry opened up remote havens that history, life or daily desolation couldn't touch.

Slowly but surely he built up a solid reputation, becoming a trustworthy moral authority as he silently bore the unbearable brunt of events, of the pain that history, empires and invaders constantly inflicted on his land. The twentieth century had brought independence to that wonderfully civilised and cultured country of his but soon it also ushered in Nazi occupation and, after the liberation from fascism, a new foreign tyranny.

Pravda vítězí—"truth prevails", claimed the Czech theologian Jan Hus, who had been betrayed and burnt alive in 1415. But a man's life is short and fragile; his strength is limited. The lives of states and empires, no matter how inert, cynical and oppressive they are, are so much longer and more resilient that it is a hopeless battle for a defenceless individual to oppose them.

The 1968 Prague Spring seemed a dream come true, the utopia of a humane socialism, the third way so feared by the two empires that would soon be itching to crush it, aware as they were of the danger it posed and of the strength generated by civilisation and freedom of spirit. It had been a short-lived dream but those few months had been enough to make up for years of anguish, repression, obtuse short-sightedness, back-stabbing informers and stifling control. A dream of his was about to come true that summer: he would translate *Doctor Zhivago*, a work he had long pursued and finally conquered through hardships worthy of a novel. His translation was almost ready but then, on a fateful August night, the invasion came—a low blow emanating from the Warsaw Pact. The black horde, the tanks, the occupiers soon set out to ban new publications and crush that sense of uncensored freedom that Alexander Dubček had tried fruitlessly to get the distant masters in Moscow—the owners of that half of the world—to accept.

During that short-lived season everything seemed possible; censorship had disappeared and new books and translations were published without the fear of proscription; people were free to talk and voice their ideas, opinions and hopes.

Being able to write and translate without any forced political or ideological bias seemed almost unreal to the people who had experienced the dark years of Gottwald, the Czech communist leader, of the Slánský show trial and of the sombre and overbearing powers that be.

Intellectuals were overwhelmed by their almost unreal freedom, so it was all the more painful to go back to order and cowardly obedience to the party's dictates, to the cultural and literary tastes of its lieutenants and of the men in charge of cultural policy.

From then on, everything would be tougher, especially for the ones who had found their own niche from where to write, to translate and to breathe, for the ones who sowed their talent, limpid gaze and taste as poets and translators in the interstices left untouched by the powers that be. There's an emblematic sentence in his diary that says much about the feeling of utter defeat and vainness of every creation he and perhaps others experienced in the new situation: "discreetly burying one's talent like shit in a sandy beach, in the dead of night."

He was the Prague man. His name was Jan Zábrana.

JAN ZÁBRANA

Fate led me to Jan Zábrana in a bookshop on the
Opletalova, in Prague, on a bright cold afternoon. The
sun was setting. I stopped to gaze at the house opposite,
its windows looking out on emptiness and the sky—the
building had collapsed except for the façade, balanced
precariously as it waited for a prop from the future. The
past had disappeared behind it and all that remained
was the faint architecture of memory, the simulacrum of
things gone by, the elegant shape of an illusion that only
daylight could dissolve. At night the windows went dark
again, nothingness coalesced beyond the façade. Nobody
would guess there was no actual house with walls and
rooms protected from the shadows. I went into the bookshop—the cavern of warmth, light and words I popped
into occasionally on my days of wandering—and roamed
the shelves with no particular book in mind. Then I
noticed a thick white volume, its shiny cover magnified
by plastic wrapping.

I read the title: *Celý život.*

Jan Zábrana.

A Whole Life.

I already knew Zábrana and his poems. This, however, was a book I'd never even picked up. It was a mint edition; the salesman told me it had been published in two parts and had quickly sold out. *Celý život* was about an era that was sombre and painful, for the writer and for many others; and in those daily memories there were traces of a past life, of the years the reader might have experienced too and that had never quite vanished.

Late that night, as I sat on my sofa with the Vltava river roaring outside, I read Zábrana's thoughts, a vital part of him which he entrusted to thin sheets of paper in order to stem defeat, the derision of things, the advancing of death on his generation leaving no chance of escape or survival. I leafed through the book, picking out pages at random and drawing closer to his later years, ever closer to the present. I got to the summer of 1980. As I read a passage I suddenly realised I was holding my breath—he was detailing a car accident from twenty years previously, a fatal crash involving Albert Camus.

THE TRUTH

The words were accurate, cutting and straight to the point.

They seemed to have been laid out on the page with mysterious, fatal sparseness.

They told of a far-off time, a great many complex events, a deadly conspiracy, the deceptiveness of things, and of how men are prone to short-sightedness.

It was all distilled into those words. An irreparable event, the death of a man that recalled the death of ancient heroes, stricken by ill luck or by jealous gods just when they were about to achieve greatness—this was the fate told and sealed in those few short, impeccable lines.

It was like a sudden, entrancing act of fate that left no room for astonishment, breath for words or memories to regret.

Everything was clear now.

The laws of the world had closed in over a man and his life.

The laws of deception and oblivion had mingled to conceal the names of the killers and the crucial events surrounding the sacrifice from history and from the fragile memory of man.

The eternity of oblivion and the darkness of time had immediately enshrouded reality, things, events and the silent occurrence of it all.

And yet, like sparks from a far-off fire with no-one to see it, the untainted words of a man managed to save what eternal darkness had been plotting to enshroud forever.

It was almost as if some mysterious justice from far away had sent a fragile, unknown witness to an unwelcoming world to make a righteous man privy to the ultimate flash of a dying truth, the pale glimmer of an unseen shipwreck, so as to preserve its traces forever.

Thus wrote Jan Zábrana in his diary in the late summer of 1980:

> I heard something very strange from a knowledgeable and well-connected man. He says the car crash that cost Camus his life in 1960 was set up by Soviet intelligence.
>
> They rigged the tyre with a tool that eventually pierced it when the car was travelling at high speed.
>
> The order was issued by the minister of internal affairs Shepilov himself as payback for the article published in *Franc-Tireur* in March 1957 in which Camus commented on the events in Hungary, explicitly attacking the minister.
>
> It seems it took the intelligence three years to carry out the order.
>
> They managed eventually and in such a way that, until today, everyone thought Camus had died because of an ordinary car crash.
>
> The man refused to tell me his source but he claimed it was completely reliable and that he knew beyond a shadow of

doubt that that was how things had played out and that they had Camus' death on their conscience.

That was all.

HONOUR AND FATE

Death begins in a mysterious instant that might appear decisive only much later; at the present moment, we are all blind and directionless; we move around sometimes thinking we know things, imagining the future, even if we're surrounded by darkness. Albert Camus had an instinct for events and he could instantly make out what it was right to fight for. Maybe at the end of 1956, in the light of those grave events, he had followed his instinct and his sense of justice without thinking about the consequences. In a way, a man of principle never dies—his beliefs outlive him. Camus was already ahead of his time, and his life—as during the Resistance years, when to him mere "survival" was secondary and, under certain conditions, unbearable. So Camus had nothing to lose and every word and move of his would give further meaning to his life—this was what mattered to him.

In late October 1956 the Soviets had bloodily crushed the Hungarian uprising. All of Europe watched impotently from the sidelines, spectators as the USSR abused its power, managing only to provide the rebels with ideological support. Camus couldn't help speaking his mind:

he let loose with all the indignation of a libertarian who refused to bow to tyranny, regardless of its colour; he was also directly appealed to by Hungarian writers as they sent out a desperate cry for help to the free thinkers of the West. Camus went out of his way to help, generously leveraging his name and moral authority. His indignant words were published throughout the international media; in Paris, the site of his struggles and land of his unbreakable freedom, he delivered memorable speeches.

He didn't just shoot down the invaders of Hungary— he also directed scathing criticism at the Soviet Foreign Minister, Dmitri T. Shepilov, who had arrogantly championed his government's actions even before the United Nations (where he was the official representative of the Soviet Union).

Twenty-four years later, Zábrana's source recalled these events down to the finest detail. These factual memories had been preserved in rooms far away from Moscow; nothing of Camus' efforts had been lost.

If we think about the massive international respect Camus garnered—he was a shoe-in for the Nobel Prize—these statements must have rubbed the Soviet leaders—and Dmitri T. Shepilov in particular—the wrong way.

Furthermore, at the time the public pronouncements of intellectuals were far more feared and heeded than today. Camus' position on the events in Hungary had really made a huge impression in Europe and across the world.

He had to be stopped, no matter how.

THE WORDS

Albert Camus had sided firmly with the Hungarian Uprising since autumn 1956. Another factor prompting his decision was the appeal by Hungarian writers to the great Western novelists and poets of the time. This was issued on 4 November 1956 and renewed on the 7 November during the tragic days of the Budapest Uprising that was crushed by invading Soviet troops. The latter would eventually capture and kill Imre Nagy, the reformist Hungarian Prime Minister guilty of opposing normalisation.

Camus answered with "*Réponse à l'appel des intellectuels hongrois*", an article published in *Franc-Tireur* on 10 November.

On 23 November, he issued a statement supporting the Hungarian uprising at a meeting of French students.

He was then interviewed on the matter by the *New York Times* on 24 February 1957.

In February 1957, *Demain* ran his article "*Le socialisme des potences*" (The socialism of the gallows).

Then, in October 1957, the *Times* published Camus's communiqué, "Appeal for Hungarian Writers", that was sent to a public meeting on the matter held in London.

Finally, the December 1958 issue of *Témoins* ran an article titled "*Encore la Hongrie*", including his foreword to *La vérité sur l'affaire Nagy* (Plon, 1958), a collection of documents and testimony refuting the charges made against Imre Nagy at his trial in Budapest.

Two speeches of Camus on the matter sparked the ire of Soviet minister Shepilov, whom he attacked directly. The first was delivered on 30 October 1956, during a meeting of the exiled Spanish Republican government; the speech was then republished in *Monde Nouveau*.

The more famous interview, quoted by Zábrana's source, took place at the Salle Wagram in Paris on 15 March 1957 and was published in *Franc-Tireur* on 18 March 1957 with the title "*Kádár a eu son jour de peur*" (Kádár has had his moment of fear). Here, Camus once again attacked Shepilov.

Camus attacked Shepilov and his comrades for ordering and covering up massacres under the guise of socialist realism, repressing writers and artists in Hungary, the Soviet Union and elsewhere, poisoning intellectual life with propaganda and crushing freedom.

Camus' words had a tremendous impact and furthered his commitment to ensuring that the Hungarian writers' fight for freedom would not be forgotten.

He was also proving to be a thorn in Moscow's side as he tirelessly brought before international public opinion the Soviet repression of Hungary.

It was no longer tolerable.

Something had to be done to stop him.

The entry in Zábrana's diary dates back to 1980. He specifically mentions Camus' speech published in *Franc-*

Tireur twenty-four years earlier and Shepilov, the minister Camus singled out for particular criticism. It is highly unlikely that he could have had such a clear recollection of an episode related to events far from the issues and harsh reality of post-Charter 77 Czechoslovakia.

It was almost certainly Zábrana's source who provided the flawlessly detailed circumstances of the event, thanks to the information he possessed.

HUNGARY

The Soviet invasion of Hungary in 1956 left European public opinion and the non-Stalinist Left aghast.

The Khrushchev Report had unveiled the true nature of Stalin's regime. The brutal and traumatic operation that followed it revealed that Moscow's methods hadn't changed one jot.

After the uprisings in East Berlin in 1953 and in Poznań in June 1956 precipitated by the deteriorating living and employment conditions of Eastern European workers, it took a mere spark in Hungary on 23 October 1956 to set off a raging fire that couldn't be contained.

That afternoon a student rally organised in support of Władysław Gomułka and the Poznań demonstrators gathered in Pest, around the statue of Hungary's national poet Sándor Petőfi, who in 1848 had inspired the launch of a popular but strongly nationalist youth organisation.

The gathering soon turned into a violent protest. The crowd headed to the House of Parliament as tens of thousands of people converged on the city centre.

The demonstrators toppled a statue of Stalin and a massive crowd assembled in front of the offices of

Hungarian Radio. The ÁVH (State Protection Authority) secret police then opened fire, leading to the first deaths among those assembled.

The central committee of the Hungarian Communist Party decided to call in Soviet troops "if they were needed" and on 24 October Imre Nagy was appointed head of the government, replacing András Hegedüs.

The intervention of Soviet troops turned the revolt into a full-blown insurrection. Weapons were handed out to civilians, police cars set on fire and the ÁVH headquarters besieged by the crowd. Workers' councils were set up in factories and a general strike was called; the working classes themselves turned out to be the staunchest defenders of the revolt, despite the Soviets' crushing superiority. The latter's forces based in Hungary consisted mostly of armoured units and were of little use in the street to street fighting that ensued.

Soviet Politburo representatives Anastas Mikoyan and Mikhail Suslov hurried to Budapest to assist the ambassador Yuri Andropov and to take stock of the situation.

On 25 October the Nagy government installed itself and János Kádár was appointed Communist Party Secretary in place of Ernő Gerő. The police and the military began siding with the rebels.

Imre Nagy parlayed with the Russians, who still saw him as a trustworthy figure and the only one capable of ending the revolt. On 28 October he managed to negotiate a cease-fire, acknowledging the national and democratic character of the insurrection and announcing the dissolution of the ÁVH as well as the imminent withdrawal of Soviet troops.

When the troops did indeed begin to withdraw, though, it turned out to be a ruse.

For a few days Hungary believed it had fended off the threat of the superpower, but the international context offered the Russians an easy pretext to move in again. It began with the Suez Canal crisis, following a joint attack against Egypt by Great Britain, France and Israel that shifted the focus of international public opinion.

On 31 October the presidium of the central committee of the CPSU authorised the invasion: fresh troops would initiate a massive attack. Thanks to the near simultaneous assault of the Western powers against Egypt, the Soviets were able to conceal their weak hand and intervene even in the face of hostile Western public opinion.

The first Soviet armoured columns reached the Hungarian border on 1 November.

Nagy demanded an explanation from Ambassador Andropov, who played down the whole affair. Mindful of the threat posed by Russian forces, however, Nagy declared Hungary's neutrality, withdrew his country from the Warsaw Pact and called on the United Nations to debate the situation and defend the declaration of independence. He realised time was short and that Hungary was being caught in a rapidly-closing vice. Soon, the excitement and enthusiasm of so many Hungarians would be replaced with terror.

On 2 November the UN debated the situation in Hungary and the following day, during further negotiations at a Soviet military base, KGB agents arrested General Pál Maléter, the military leader of the Hungarian delegation.

On 4 November the Soviet Red Army, formerly a liberating army, invaded and crushed Hungary's national freedom, deploying a staggering 4,000 tanks in the process.

Kádár, who had flown to Moscow, quickly returned and in a radio-broadcast announced the formation of a new government.

The workers' councils resisted heroically despite being thoroughly outnumbered.

Unlike the first offensive, in October, this time the Soviets also deployed infantry, bombers and artillery—it was a full-blown strategic military assault.

The industrial and working-class areas of Budapest resisted stoically, faring better than the army itself, which had for all intents and purposes been decapitated.

On 10 November the workers' councils called for a cease-fire, their last shred of hope seemingly gone.

Kádár formed a new government, backdating its existence to 3 November so he could claim that a legitimately ruling government had called on the Soviet troops to intervene.

Imre Nagy and other members of the government had fled to the Yugoslav embassy, hoping to be granted political asylum. Little did they know that Khrushchev had flown to the Brionian Islands to convince Tito to hand over the fugitives.

On 22 November they left the embassy with a safe-conduct pass from Kádár guaranteeing them a secure "return home."

Instead, they were arrested by the Soviets and immediately deported.

Imre Nagy, General Pál Maléter and journalist and politician Miklós Gimes were tried, found guilty of treason and, on 16 June 1958, hanged.

It was only on 16 June 1989, thirty-one years later, that Imre Nagy and the other men were given a proper burial and their names cleared.

THE APPEAL

On 4 November 1956, as Soviet troops were already besieging Hungary, Radio Budapest broadcast a message to intellectuals worldwide:

> Poets, writers, men of knowledge from all over the world— Hungary's writers are calling on you. Heed our appeal. We are fighting on the barricades for our country's freedom, for Europe's and for humankind's dignity. We're going to die. Do not let our sacrifice be in vain. At the supreme hour and in the name of a massacred nation we call on you, Camus, Malraux, Mauriac, Russell, Jaspers, Einaudi, Eliot, Koestler, Madariaga, Jiménez, Kazantzakis, Lagerkvist, Laxness, Hesse and many other fighters of the spirit. Take action.

On 8 November Camus was wired the text of the appeal and set to work right away. He called on left liberal Georges Altman, the editor-in-chief of his favourite daily, *Franc-Tireur*. On 9 November the paper published the Hungarians' appeal and the following day it ran Camus' piece.

To Camus, the tragic invasion of Hungary was tantamount to the fascist destruction of the Spanish Republic twenty years earlier—an event he had spoken of just a few days before, on 30 October, during a public speech in honour of Spanish historian and diplomat Salvador de Madariaga. On that occasion Camus had also made his first, scathing denunciation of the Soviet Foreign Minister Dmitri Shepilov, the man who would eventually put out a contract on him.

SALLE WAGRAM, 15 MARCH 1957

On 30 October, during his speech in honour of Salvador de Madariaga, Camus publicly attacked Shepilov and referred to the "savage intervention by Soviet troops."

The worst massacre was still to come, though. The Soviet armed forces would be unleashed in early November, causing countless deaths, without the slightest regard for Hungarian national sovereignty. It was the outcome of the Yalta Conference—each of the superpowers (the United States, the Soviet Union and the United Kingdom) was to have carte blanche within its sphere of influence and could carry out the most duplicitous acts without having to worry about other countries stepping in.

Latin American and some European nations paid an equally high price when the Western powers began to doubt their fealty, and cruel, fascist-like dictatorships were foisted upon them, till the mid-Seventies in Europe and much later in Latin America. Underhand terrorist campaigns, strategies of cruelty, were launched to manipulate public opinion.

Events as grave as those in Hungary were not to occur again for decades. The 1968 invasion of Czechoslovakia was much less bloody; on the other side, only the cruelty of the military coup organised by the CIA in Chile in 1973 against Salvador Allende and the legitimate Unidad Popular government are comparable.

For most of 1957, Camus made sure that international public opinion did not forget the Hungarian tragedy. We have already mentioned his interview with the *New York Times* on 24 February, the article in the magazine *Demain* in February entitled "The Socialism of the Gallows" and his contribution in the *Times* that October, "Appeal to Hungarian writers".

The protest sent shockwaves around the world and Camus' stinging reproaches were by now proving too much to bear for the men who green-lit the military intervention and now had to defend it before the world's institutions. Global public opinion was still well aware of that dreadful deed. But only one man tirelessly rubbed the invaders' noses in the disgrace of that massacre: Albert Camus.

According to Jan Zábrana and his source, that scathing speech at the Salle Wagram cost Camus his life.

Indeed, it seems that after it Shepilov personally ordered the KGB to get rid of him.

The speech was the straw that broke the camel's back: first the personal attack on 30 October, then the response to the Hungarian writers, his stance with the United Nations, and his tireless efforts worldwide. Camus just wouldn't let it go.

Camus was still championing Hungary in 1958, when he penned a scathing foreword to *The Truth on the Nagy Affair*, after the head of the rebel government, Imre Nagy, was gratuitously executed.

THE IMAGES

Here, before our own eyes, are the tense, dense images of the place where Albert Camus crashed. Almost everything seems beyond time, oblivion and the fatal fading of memory. With no sound, the scene is suspended and ghostly; the faces of the onlookers show surprise, respect and the certainty they are witnessing an event that is beyond their grasp, that transcends the instant and is already moving towards history, as part of a greater design. Death lingers among those trees, on that road, in the wreck that seems to preserve the energy of the crash, the tremendous power of the impact and destruction. The events have already occurred and yet still linger on at the scene of the catastrophe; everything seems to be vibrating and moving along the imperceptible trajectory of fate: a secret energy holds together the elements of the disaster, the inanimate objects in disarray, the crash, the blistering detachment; everything still remains, frozen and suspended by the energy of the tragedy, in the invisible geometry that connects every slightest fragment of the devastation.

All of a sudden a policeman, almost violating the sacral motionlessness of dead things, inspects a tyre torn from within—probably the real cause of the tragedy.

And so we remember the first headlines of the newspapers at the time that claimed the tyre was the cause of the accident, just like a recent report by *Mediapart* that confidently pointed to it as the culprit of the deadly crash. Jan Zábrana's words echo louder than ever: "They rigged the tyre with a tool that eventually pierced it when the car was travelling at high speed. ... They managed eventually and in such a manner that, until today, everyone thought Camus had died because of an ordinary car crash."

THE FATAL JOURNEY

Camus' biography by Herbert Lottman contains surely the most accurate and best-documented account of the accident that cost Camus his life. Lottman gained the trust of Janine Gallimard, the wife of the publisher who also died in the crash. She and the couple's daughter were also in the car on that fateful day. She often invited Lottman over to the apartment above the offices of the publishing house for a chat. Mrs Gallimard's trust was also instrumental in retrieving small episodes and memories that would otherwise have been lost.

On 3 January 1960, the Gallimards and Camus left Lourmarin in the late morning. They stopped for a quick lunch at Orange.

At the time there was no motorway they could take, so they travelled along what was virtually the only feasible route: first Route Nationale 7 from Avignon to Lyon, then Route Nationale 6 across Burgundy: Mâcon, Chalon, Avallon, Auxerre and Sens. From Sens they would take Route Nationale 5 (via Fontainebleau) to Paris. So their route was very easy to predict—and to monitor.

The travellers left Route Nationale 6 just before Mâcon to spend the night and dine in Thoissey, where there was a very nice hotel restaurant they knew well, Le Chapon Fin, which boasted two Michelin stars.

They had booked some rooms (something that would have been easy to intercept), since many holidaymakers were heading home and the main roads and restaurants were bound to be packed.

Madame Blanc, the owner of the hotel, kept Camus' registration form—perhaps the last document he ever filled in and signed.

Lottman tells us that after a short rest, the travellers had dinner in Thoissey, the event soon turning into something special: it was Anne Gallimard's eighteenth birthday and Camus celebrated it with warmth and affection.

Madame Blanc noticed the guests were happy and relaxed.

Camus spoke about his writing for the theatre and tried to convince Michel Gallimard to let his daughter take part in the plays. Gallimard didn't want her to become an actress but Camus was sure he could get her involved in his stage projects: he and Anne trusted each other implicitly.

After a lavish dinner the four spent a peaceful night; the car, however, was unguarded. It is quite likely that it was sabotaged during the night so as to cause the fatal crash.

The next morning the travellers had breakfast and left the hotel between nine and ten.

According to Janine Gallimard a curious exchange took place in the car. Michel Gallimard wanted to take out a life insurance policy. Camus pointed out that two men as prone to tuberculosis as them were unlikely to be granted coverage. Michel thought often about death and had no qualms speaking about it; he said he wanted to die before his wife because he couldn't live without her. Eventually, he and Camus agreed that, if they died together, they wanted to be embalmed and kept in Janine's living room so she could speak to them every day. Janine said it was a horrible thought and she would rather move out of the flat.

The car rolled along at a moderate pace. Even though Michel was keen on speed, Janine didn't want him to drive too fast; even Camus reprimanded him whenever he pushed it too far.

Around lunchtime they reached Sens, a town dominated by a spectacular Gothic cathedral.

Along the main road (which was part of the Route Nationale) was the Hôtel de Paris et de la Poste, which also had a nice restaurant.

Camus was familiar with it and led the way.

The four sat in a large room with a fireplace and wood-panelled walls (according to Janine). They ordered *boudin noir aux pommes de reinette* (blood sausage with rennet apples) and a bottle of Beaujolais (according to Monsieur Sandré, the owner of the place).

They didn't stay long and were soon on their way again. Camus had an appointment with a friend, María Casares, in Paris that evening and didn't want to be late.

They carried on along Route Nationale 5, which passed through several villages after Sens. At the time the road had three lanes, the middle one being used to overtake, and was bordered for long stretches by magnificent—and dangerous—plane trees.

They passed Pont-sur-Yonne and drew closer to Petit Villeblevin.

The four chatted on; Janine Gallimard was sure they weren't speeding. Suddenly Gallimard exclaimed "*Merde!*"

Janine, who was in the back with Anne and their dog, Floc, heard nothing else. She felt a sudden swerve and then as if something were collapsing under the car.

According to passing drivers and to another driver waiting to merge, the car zigzagged in the middle of the carriageway before crashing into a tree and ricocheting against another one thirteen metres further down, folding up like an accordion.

A witness in another car claimed he had been overtaken by the Facel Vega at 150 km per hour. He said the car was "dancing a waltz" and the crash was "like an explosion."

One version had the speedometer stuck at 145 km per hour; another had it back to nought.

As Lottman mentions, "not even the experts could explain that catastrophic accident on a straight stretch nine metres wide and with very little traffic."

Lottman also claims that the photos that were taken "showed a fifty-plus metre tear in the asphalt". What caused the damage to the asphalt and which part of the car could have been involved?

The wreckage was scattered over a 150-metre radius.

The bumper and the dashboard of the Vega had been ripped off and landed nine metres from the remains of the car (mainly the rear); the radiator grille was on the other side of the road and a single wheel lay in the carriageway.

The women had ended up in a field and were virtually unharmed; Anne was twenty metres from the car and caked in mud; Floc, the dog, had disappeared and would never be found.

Michel Gallimard was in shock. When he was lifted from the ground he was bleeding profusely.

Camus crashed through the windshield, shattering his skull, crushing his chest and fracturing his spinal cord. The passenger seat had no safety belt, hence Camus' injuries were the worst.

Gallimard was whisked to hospital. He couldn't remember anything; in the ambulance he asked Janine if he had been driving. Later, he was transferred to a hospital in Paris. He was believed to have a crushed spleen but died of a brain haemorrhage on 10 January while undergoing surgery.

Janine was diagnosed with a hairline fracture to a cervical vertebrae and had to wear a neck brace for months.

Camus' corpse was handed over to the municipality of Villeblevin. Citizens and friends gathered the next day to mourn him. The pied-noir writer Emmanuel Roblès insisted on lifting the black funeral drape to see his friend's face one last time. "Under the light of a bare bulb he had the face of a sleeping person—someone who was very, very tired. A long scratch ran across his forehead, like a final line drawn across a page."

The Minister of Culture, André Malraux, who was also a friend of Camus', held a commemorative speech and said: "For more than twenty years Camus was one with his obsession for justice. We bid farewell to one of the people thanks to whom France is always in the hearts of men."

When Camus' body was buried in Lourmarin, a wreath was sent with the words: "To a friend of Hungary. From exiled Hungarians."

THE SITE OF THE CRASH

The French National Audiovisual Institute's silent footage from the day of the crash has become a precious relic, much like that of a sunken ship from which unexpected fragments suddenly emerge. We can witness the devastation, the scene of the crash without its victims or the sudden tragedy that faded out, leaving a debris-scattered stage.

The car was crumpled up against the second tree, having broken in two. The front part had shattered; the rear was virtually dangling from the tree but had somehow preserved its shape, saving the lives of the two female passengers.

The front grille, with the fatal words Facel and Vega on either side next to the headlights, lies on the other side of the road; it was likely torn off during the first crash.

The engine lies precariously on the hard shoulder; a part of it might be missing, having been snapped like a toy and left on the wet asphalt. Close by are the increasingly minute shards of the headlights, shattered by the violent impact.

The camera turns away from the car wreck, pans across the road, frames the engine and then slowly pans down to film the traces on the asphalt. After crashing into the first tree, the Facel Vega shot across the carriageway before coming to its final, deadly halt.

So the first crash happened on the left side of the road, contra the flow of traffic. The driver and front passenger suffered a first violent impact against the steering wheel and the windshield; the front of the car was shattered. The car then spun out of control, somehow gouging the tarmac with a very sharp part of the vehicle, did a half-turn and then crashed into the second tree on the right side of the road, the front passenger seat—where Camus was travelling—bearing the brunt of the impact.

The wreck was almost wrapped around the tree, as was the front axle, with its one remaining wheel; the impact on the passenger side was devastating.

In the 5 January edition of *Combat*, Camus' favourite daily, it was stated that Camus' corpse was wedged between the seat and the car body (on the side of the second impact).

A second, commonly accepted version is that Camus' head smashed through the windscreen when the second crash occurred, effectively snapping his neck.

So the second crash was sideways but the car had spun on itself and was almost back-to-front, so Camus' body had almost been thrown backwards.

He was the only one still in the vehicle when the second impact occurred; the other three had probably been thrown from the car as it hurtled towards the second tree.

Combat and then *Le Monde* hypothesised that the accident had been caused by the rear left tyre exploding.

The press in general seemed to agree.

The footage shows a gendarme lifting and inspecting the ruptured wheel and part of the suspension still dangling from it; it was presumably the front left tyre, which had been struck violently during the first, almost head-on collision. The tyre is severely damaged on its inner rim—an area that generally does not suffer from wear and tear or punctures. So what caused that deep laceration?

Did that sabotaged wheel cause the car to spin out of control?

Zábrana and his source state it clearly: "They rigged the tyre with a tool that eventually pierced it when the car was travelling at high speed."

The culprits would have had another chance to sabotage the car when Camus and the Gallimards had stopped for lunch at the Hôtel de Paris et de la Poste in Sens.

Looking at a map of the area gives one the shivers: the scene of the crash is just a few kilometres after Sens, at a point where the car had probably reached cruising speed and hence was travelling faster than during the earlier part of the journey.

In the letter he sent to María Casares from Lourmarin a few days earlier, Camus told her he would be travelling by car; hence, he had already decided a few days beforehand that he wouldn't take the train.

Maybe María Casares told other people and the news reached an informer; in any case, Camus had spoken to others over the phone about his plans to return with the Gallimards. A mere phone tap would have been enough to make his every move known in advance to eavesdroppers.

During the March 1997 episode of the French broadcast *Cercle de minuit*, which was dedicated to María Casares, mention was made of the letter Camus had written to her promising he'd be in Paris in time for dinner on 4 January unless he had any car-related problems.

Maybe he was merely thinking of a possible delay but in hindsight those words take on an entirely different meaning.

THE KGB'S ACTIONS IN CAMUS' TIMES

Towards the end of his life Camus often spoke out against Stalinism and denounced the Soviet invasion of Hungary. During those years, the USSR's secret services (KGB) were taken over by two ruthless men who made no qualms about killing off the Soviet Union's real or assumed enemies at home and abroad.

From 1954 to 1958 its leader was State Security General Ivan Serov, who oversaw the Hungarian invasion under orders from Khrushchev. His men boycotted talks between the Hungarian army, the rebels and the Russian troops, and executed a sneak arrest of the head of the Hungarian negotiators, General Pál Maléter, who was eventually hanged along with Imre Nagy. Khrushchev himself tasked Serov with overseeing the final invasion of Hungary in early November after the first Soviet intervention failed.

During Serov's years in charge, foreign operations were constant and many anti-Soviet émigrés were kidnapped. These operations weren't new, since defectors or self-exiled dissidents had often been killed in the past.

In 1937, the NKVD had assassinated Ignatz Reiss (or Ignace Poretsky) in Lausanne, Switzerland. He had defected after the Stalinists tortured to death the Spanish POUM founder, Andreu Nin Pérez, having written to Stalin telling him he no longer wanted to share the highest Soviet honour with the same men who were killing off the workers and the best representatives of the Revolution.

General Walter Krivitsky, a friend of Reiss', had defected shortly after him and was killed at the Bellevue Hotel in Washington in February 1941. A fake suicide was staged.

Lev Sedov, the son of Leon Trotsky, died under suspicious circumstances in Paris after undergoing surgery due to appendicitis. His father, the great revolutionary defeated by Stalin, was murdered in Mexico in August 1940 by Ramón Mercader, at Moscow's behest.

Moving forward to Camus' time, in 1952 Walter Linse, who had fled East Germany in 1947 and headed the Free Jurists, was kidnapped in West Berlin, taken to East Berlin, tried and imprisoned. In this case the operation was carried out by East German intelligence operatives following KGB orders. Linse was seen as a dangerously committed man due to his public activities abroad.

In 1953 Bohumil Laušman, a Czechoslovakian émigré since 1947, was kidnapped in Vienna by Czechoslovakian agents backed by the Soviets. The Russians provided a diplomatic car to safely carry the abductee through Vienna and the Austrian zone under Soviet control all the way to the border.

In those years the KGB focused on members of the NTS (*Narodno Trudovoy Soyouz*), the National Alliance of Russian Solidarists, which operated abroad among émigrés who opposed the Soviet regime.

The NTS head Rudolf Trushnovic was kidnapped in Berlin in April 1954 and sent back to the USSR. The same fate befell NTS member, Valeri Tremmel, who was kidnapped in Linz, Austria, in June 1954 before being returned home and imprisoned.

In February 1954 a hit was put out on Georgi Okolovich, one of the NTS's leaders. The murder was to be carried out by two DDR agents under the supervision of KGB member Nikolai Khokhlov. Overcome by remorse and backed by his wife (who was eventually tried and sentenced), Khokhlov went to Okolovich and revealed the plans to kill him; he then defected and turned himself in to the Western secret services.

Khokhlov's revelations provided the CIA with much information about the KGB and its secret structures for neutralizing Soviet enemies. In particular, they learned of two separate laboratories: one for developing special weapons and explosives and another for designing highly effective poisons and drugs that could quickly eliminate targets without leaving any traces, even in the event of an autopsy. As we will see, these two labs provided the tools for the two killings abroad ordered soon afterwards by Bohdan Stashinski.

Khokhlov himself was almost killed during an anti-communist meeting in Frankfurt in 1957. He was poisoned with a mysterious substance, believed to be thallium, a very rare and dangerous radioactive compound similar to polonium, which was also used in London years later to poison Alexander Litvinenko's tea. Despite the initial scepticism of the British authorities, just before he died, Litvinenko managed to tell them his suspicions about being poisoned, and so while the doctors treating him were able to locate the cause, they couldn't save his life.

Khokhlov did survive and recover. He moved to the US, where he stayed until his death. He was pardoned by Russian president Boris Yeltsin and allowed to visit Moscow in the 1990s.

In March 1955 Lisa Stein, a reporter for Berlin-based American broadcaster RIAS (Radio in the American Sector), was almost kidnapped in West Berlin.

She had met up in a café with a friend who was in fact a Soviet agent. Before leaving, the friend offered her a sweet laced with scopolamine, a substance which should have affected her while Stein headed home. The plan was to follow her by car and, once she fell unconscious, kidnap her and take her to East Berlin.

But by the time the scopolamine kicked in, Stein was already at her own front door. Her neighbours hurried to intervene, effectively saving her. For a few days she was in a critical condition and the doctors couldn't figure out what had caused her illness; she eventually recovered.

When Serov was succeeded as Chairman of the KGB by Alexander Shelepin in 1958, it was clear that the intent was to carry on along the same lines. The executions abroad continued and aggressiveness was ramped up; Serov took charge of the GRU, the military foreign intelligence service.

Shelepin soon became known among his collaborators as *Zhelezni Shurik*, the Steel Alexander. He was renowned for his cruelty and ruthlessness in the pursuit of his goals. Years later he plotted to oust the first secretary of the CPSU, Nikita Khrushchev, his former mentor, as head of the USSR, in favour of the neo-Stalinists led by Leonid Brežhnev, who would soon have him demoted to a harmless post, fearful of his influence, ambition and the threat he posed.

Under his command the previous precautions by which foreign operations were usually carried out by agents belonging to satellite countries under KGB supervision were thrown out.

Shelepin directed the KGB until 1961. The car crash that cost Camus his life happened on 4 January 1960. Camus held the speech that led to a hit being put out him on 15 March 1957, when for the umpteenth time he spoke out against Soviet foreign minister Shepilov.

As Jan Zábrana wrote, "The hit was put out by the Minister of Internal Affairs Shepilov himself ... It is rumoured it took the secret services three years to carry out the order. They eventually did, and executed the plan flawlessly."

A 1964 CIA document concerning the KGB's executions abroad (the document was declassified in 1993) states: "The killings of emigrated leaders have been carried out so skilfully that it seems the victims have died of natural causes."

In those years, two more killings were carried out in Munich. The victims were intellectual Lev Rebet and political leader Stepan Bandera, both of them top representatives of the Ukrainian opposition abroad.

In Rebet's case, it seemed he died of a heart attack or a stroke. Bandera's death is shrouded in mystery, however his condition at the time of death suggested he was poisoned.

The truth would probably have never emerged if, on the evening of 12 August 1961, just a few hours before the Berlin Wall was built, a man anxious to get in touch with the American Sector authorities hadn't handed himself over to the West Berlin police.

The man was Bohdan Stashinski, a.k.a. Julius (or, alternatively, Josef) Lehmann, a KGB agent, along with his wife Inge Pohl, who was the ultimate cause of his defection. The two had taken advantage of the preparation for the funeral of their baby, who had died while just a few months old, in the outskirts of East Berlin, to flee from the KGB, who had grown suspicious of them and wouldn't let them leave the Soviet Union.

They left from the back door of the house of Stashinski's father-in-law in the suburb of Dallgow, walked all the way to the village of Falkensee and took a cab to East Berlin crossing the Friedrichstrasse checkpoint, which they passed thanks to Lehmann's ID. They then took the S-Bahn to the Gesundbrunnen stop, the first in West Berlin, avoiding any more paper checks.

When the American agents heard Stashinski's story they realised they had in their hands a key figure who was also responsible for major, unsolved crimes. Stashinski provided them with all the details—eventually corroborated by investigations—admitting he had killed Lev Rebet and Stepan Bandera under KGB orders.

He had used a special weapon loaded with untraceable cyanide capsules. The weapon came from the Soviet labs Khokhlov had mentioned. It was a 7-inch cylinder weighing no more than 200 grams. Rebet had been killed with a single-loaded one, Bandera with a double-loaded one. It was placed very close to the victim's face to spray the cyanide which, once inhaled, paralysed the arteries shuttling blood to the brain; this caused a heart attack or cerebral paralysis and the victim would die within one or two minutes. In the next five minutes the poison would dissolve and the arteries would go back to normal, so no trace of the deadly substance could be found.

Before killing Rebet, Stashinski and his emissary carrying the weapon tested it on a dog in East Berlin. They tied it up, sprayed it and it died without making a sound after two or three minutes of unspeakable pain.

Stashinski had been given a number of pills to take before using the spray in order to protect himself in case he accidentally breathed in any of the cyanide.

On 12 October 1957, after locating Rebet and stalking him for three days, Stashinski moved in. He entered the building where the offices of Ukrainian opposition paper *Suchasna Ukraina*, edited by Rebet himself, were located and waited for him on the first floor. When Rebet arrived he headed up the stairs; Stashinski slowly went down with the weapon concealed in a newspaper. When Rebet was just a couple of steps from him, Stashinski unloaded the cyanide right in his face and carried on down without looking back and left the building. Writhing in pain, Rebet managed to take just a couple more steps before dying in the arms of one of his colleagues.

The killing had been performed flawlessly. Rebet was believed to have died of a sudden heart attack.

After tossing the weapon into a canal, Stashinski took a train to Frankfurt, where he spent the night. He then caught a plane to East Berlin and headed to the KGB head offices in Karlshorst.

Killing Bandera had been a longer, more delicate affair.

Meanwhile, Shelepin had replaced Serov at the head of the KGB but the projects and orders issued under the former carried on all the same.

Stepan Bandera, the head of the Ukrainian nationalist organisation OUN and former domestic collaborator with the Nazis during the Second World War, was a man of action. During the war he had organised the Nachtigall (Nightingale) Battalion of the Ukrainian Legion, allied with the Nazis, as well as the UPA, the armed wing of the OUN. After being imprisoned in the Sachsenhausen concentration camp for insubordination to the Germans, he had been freed in 1944 so that he could work against the Soviets.

Bandera lived under an assumed name; moreover his well-trained organisation was said to have eliminated a number of Ukrainian émigrés suspected of being informers.

Stashinski had painstakingly staked him out, eventually locating him during a trip to the Netherlands, where Bandera had spoken at a friend's funeral. He had then carefully followed him to Munich to figure out where the best place would be to kill him.

He eventually chose the building where Bandera lived under the name Poppel. Stashinski easily managed to duplicate the key to the building. He would go in and wait for his victim, a dangerous man.

On 15 October 1959, two years after the killing of Rebet, just as Bandera pulled up in his Opel and headed to the garage, Stashinski entered the building. He went upstairs and tried to figure out whether his target, who lived on the third floor, would use the lift. A woman on her way up almost forced him to abort the operation. When Bandera approached the entry door carrying a bag of groceries in his right arm, Stashinski went down the entrance ramp towards him. Bandera opened the door with his left hand and held it open with his foot. Stashinski distracted him by asking if the lock was working and then unloaded the content of two cyanide capsules in his face before vanishing.

Bandera was found in a pool of blood on the mezzanine between the second and third floor. A number of strange bruises on his face led investigators to believe he had been poisoned.

Stashinski, meanwhile, followed his usual route through Frankfurt and the next day he was in East Berlin, where his bosses awaited him enthusiastically.

Despite the positive outcome of the operation and the accolades and honours he received from his superiors, things changed very soon when Stashinski declared he wanted to marry his German partner, Inge Pohl.

Having failed to make him change his mind, the KGB leaders grudgingly approved the marriage but demanded that his wife join the organisation and move to the USSR.

After putting up a lot of resistance, Pohl accepted the conditions imposed on her husband. Right from the outset, however, she tried to convince him to defect to the West. She never quite managed to adapt to Soviet life and when she became pregnant insisted on giving birth in her homeland, asking her husband to abandon his.

Given the growing distrust of the KGB leadership, who constantly had the couple monitored, Stashinski seized the opportunity afforded by the tragic death of his newborn son and caught up with his wife in East Berlin. With her help he eventually managed to defect to the West.

The KGB's activities abroad carried on in later years as well. In London in 1978, the pacifist Bulgarian writer Georgi Markov was killed. He had moved to the West a few years earlier and broadcast reports for the BBC World Service and Radio Free Europe. His only fault was having mocked and satirised the Eastern Bloc regimes, especially that of Bulgaria.

On 7 September, while he was waiting for the bus on Waterloo Bridge, he felt a sharp pain in his calf. He noticed the man behind him pick up an umbrella and then hurry across the street and hail a cab. When Markov reached his office his calf was still aching and he noticed there was a small red dot which was giving him pain. That evening he developed a fever and went to hospital. He died three days later due to ricin poisoning.

A 1.7 mm microsphere of platinum and iridium was found in his calf; two cavities of the sphere still contained traces of ricin. The sphere probably had a coating that kept the poison in and dissolved with bodily heat, thereby releasing the ricin into the bloodstream. At the time there was no antidote to ricin.

It was assumed that the sophisticated bullet had been shot from the umbrella.

Ten days earlier, in the Paris underground, another Bulgarian émigré, Vladimir Kostov, had been hit by an identical bullet shot from a bag. The man came down with a fever but survived because the microsphere—which was similar to the one that had killed Markov—had lost most of its poison during its trajectory.

A few years later, two high-ranking Soviet intelligence agents who defected to the West, Oleg Kalugin and Oleg Gordievsky, confirmed that the murder had been planned and carried out with the support of the KGB.

Thus there is no doubting what was the Soviet Union's policy in the Cold War against those who damaged its image abroad, and that the Russians had developed sophisticated techniques for ridding themselves of inconvenient people—not necessarily dangerous enemies but sometimes mere dissidents.

Albert Camus could cause a thousand times more damage to the Soviet Union's image than any activist, intellectual or émigré from Russia, Ukraine or Bulgaria. His tireless campaign on behalf of the Hungarian rebels cast no end of discredit on the land of "real socialism", particularly coming from a left-wing writer who was so widely respected and admired for his intellectual honesty. It is only natural to think, then, that the USSR blacklisted Camus and planned on silencing him for good.

As we have seen, the Soviets went to great lengths to ensure they were never held responsible for assassinations and made such murders seem like accidents or death by natural causes.

Maybe it was for this very reason that, as Zábrana says, it took them almost three years to get rid of Camus. "They managed eventually and in such a way that, until today, everyone thought Camus had died because of an ordinary car crash."

TIME

It has been such a long time.

Silence and oblivion have inexorably covered up those days and events without anyone ever really going beyond superficial appearances or scratching the thin, deceptive surface of things.

And yet, someone knew. Who knows how many knew. But no-one ever spoke up.

The whole world and life itself closed in on those passing deaths, even though the loss was staggering: that fearless voice with no master and no respect for the darkest and most disgraceful acts carried out by France and the powers that be would never again utter his crystalclear, piercing words that thirsted for the truth. It was a massive loss and yet someone must have celebrated it in the remote chambers of power, where Camus' words had always angered the powerful.

It has been such a long time. Silence and oblivion have inexorably covered up those days and events.

The establishment wants subjects who don't ask too many questions. You can let them vote and enjoy what looks like a smattering of freedom; but the trickeries of power, the basic laws that rule armies, finance and areas of influence are unchanging and unfathomable to most. Real power and real decisions are confined to a sphere that neither the masses nor individuals can even touch.

That man dared to shatter the logic of power and domination; that man was a threat wherever he went, in whatever direction he turned his fixed, alert, piercing gaze.

His words lashed out like so many whips. He could stir the conscience of those numbed by daily deception, by the ongoing theft of freedom, rights and information. He sought the truth of things, the human truth of the righteous who can recognise injustice, trickery, demagogy and tyranny.

His precious words would stand forever in his books; but without reading them, the future would move on in a vacuum and habitual arbitrary power would be unmatched; the future would be handed over to silence, to the secret hoarding of profit, to invasions and to murders, without a real voice like Camus to take a stand against it all, to uncover mysteries and defend us all.

THE PAGE

From the page penned by Jan Zábrana there springs an invisible, secret, unquestionable certainty—there is something in the indissoluble fabric of words and events that incessantly propagates into the present the simple evidence of the truth, the unbiased list of things as they happened, the fatal, irreparable sequence of an order, of some accurate moves, of a tragedy from which there is no return.

Very few have read that page.

You can't help being moved by it; you can't escape those plain, almost hypnotic words, that concatenation of events, that cold, cruel and unbreakable logic.

Everything has happened. And that's how it happened.

The certainty of the words arises—a slow, fatal, tragic certainty that never gives in, an inner awareness of an endless delay and of a truth that is perceptible, albeit hidden and almost buried by time.

By chance, a righteous man learned of that truth.

There was very little he could do. But he couldn't keep it to himself. And if his spoken word was fated to fade away into silence, then he would entrust it to writing and to time.

The very time that had choked him would one day perhaps redeem him; and those lines, those pages would see the light, life would strike them and the eyes of living men would read them; so he had to entrust that truth to time and to the future, until someone would bring air and light to his words—someone who could recognise their worth and confide in their truthfulness. Even the tanks, then, would be powerless faced with the power of his words and their unstoppable, unbreakable dance.

Jan Zábrana was calling from that room more removed than a prison, locked up in a miserable time, in a broken life, so that someone would come from the future and understand his words, the dignity of his pain and of his defeat.

Somehow he still calls us from afar with a confident voice and bestows his gaze, his trust and the only hope he has left upon us. We can't betray him—we mustn't betray him. He lives on in our gaze and in our ability to understand his gift to us.

He never wrote lightly—he wanted to save what was worthy of his time and show us everything that the powers that be uplifted or destroyed on a whim and with obtuse stubbornness.

Albert Camus was a fair man and Jan Zábrana saw him as a blood brother. He couldn't keep quiet now that he knew the truth—he had to give it to us, whole and bare in its ice-cold precision, in that geometric and fatal concatenation of events.

Jan Zábrana was tired and disillusioned. He knew that it might all be for nought; he knew that wrongs were never righted and that tormentors always won. But he couldn't keep quiet—he had to tell us what he knew, what the world didn't know and might never know.

He was lucid and precise and didn't use a word too many. He tells things and the facts come to life before our eyes, the darkness of the past dissolves and we can see how the death machine worked to perfection, how the fatal effect was preceded by a cause, how fate simply stood by and watched the sombre manoeuvres of men.

It wasn't destiny, the symmetry of the absurd, the fate of heroes—it was a sordid machination, a blind mechanism of death that silenced the word of a righteous man, a man who refused to sell out or become a servant, a man capable of showing the world the daily despicable acts of those in power, regardless of who they were.

After the outrage of death, the supreme ridicule of deception and silence had come.

No, he couldn't keep quiet and leave the killers in the comfortable shadow of oblivion, safe from punishment and infamy, rewarded for a vile act, defended by darkness and by everyone's indolence.

It was too much.

PRAGUE

Perhaps someone in Prague knew.

Sure, Jan Zábrana had left behind friends, acquaintances, people who had somehow kept up with his life, his silent fight, his resistance to the times, to infamy, to betrayal. Most importantly, he had left behind the person dearest to him, the one who had looked after him and was always understanding throughout his life: his wife Marie.

Her name comes with an aura of incomparable esteem and respect. Her rigour, her dignity, her precious contribution to Czech culture make her an almost revered figure.

She is known as a limpid, utterly trustworthy person. She could help me understand and maybe give me the key to Jan Zábrana's lost world.

But I wanted to do more than just investigate that grey area that had thrived in the shadow of power during the regime and that was bound to still have its web of influences and subtle pattern of motives.

There was, in particular, a man I could turn to for delicate matters. He had lived in Prague for ages and had prospered since the Cold War thanks to his family being tied in with the party and thus able to maintain international relationships that were somehow tolerated. I knew him vicariously but I was aware of his relationships with the old secret services; his innate inclination to be informed on everything made him the ideal person from whom to source news and maybe obtain new contacts.

I managed to get his private number and I called him. A cold, distant voice answered, echoing with thorough self-confidence, as if he owned a superior knowledge of things and people.

He recognised me and said: "I somehow knew you'd call me one day. What can I do for you?"

I told him I'd read a very interesting story that might involve people from the previous government. Given his experience, I wanted to tell him that story and ask him if he knew about it. He seemed quite interested and his voice changed, becoming more trusting.

"Come visit me" he said. "You know where I live. If I can, I'll tell you what I know. Come tomorrow at five."

THE CONVERSATION

When I was led into the large living room he was at the window. He turned to greet me. "I never get tired of watching the city from here" he said almost to himself.

The room looked out over Malá Strana and you could easily see Staré Město. The roofs and domes were almost dazzling in the afternoon light.

He told me to take a seat.

"So tell me, what have you learned and what might I know?"

I tried to tell him the story in the most enticing way I could, so as to grab his interest.

He gazed at me, squinting occasionally as if to peer into my mind to see if I knew more than I was letting on. He didn't say a word, not even when I was done.

He rubbed his chin very thoughtfully. Then he got up and went to the window as if to check something. He sat down again and looked at me. A strange light flashed through his eyes. He smiled.

"You've found a great story. Who knows—maybe that's what really happened. The masses don't know what's going on above them. And sometimes they deserve to be kept in the dark. The motives of the dominant need not be explained to the dominated. Sure, it's been a long time. Some drugs and poisons lose their effectiveness after a while. Maybe your story is like an expired drug. And expired drugs can be harmful. So don't go telling it left, right and centre.

I had heard something of the kind, too. But you never know in such cases. I can't remember whether our men were involved in that operation. I can't rule it out. In any case, the order definitely didn't come from us—we know quite well who was in charge. But we might have played a major role—after all, the mind does all the thinking but it can't do much without an arm. And we always were a very, very reliable arm.

A lot of our technicians went abroad at the time. They were very skilled and reliable. They could've pulled off a tricky operation of that kind. In fact, there's this close acquaintance of mine who dealt with that sort of stuff. And the funny thing is that he hasn't quite retired yet. I guess you never really can retire from that line of work."

He smiled again.

"I'll call him and tell him about this conjecture of yours and the note you found. I can't promise you anything but I reckon he'd know if anything went down. In fact, I think there are very few things now that he *doesn't* know about."

He really stressed that *doesn't*.

"Thank you" I said. "All I want is the truth—I have no wish to harm anyone." He almost burst out laughing.

"In that case you really are a threat—to yourself and to others. You know the Persian saying—well, you don't count the teeth of a gift horse. Anyway, I'll call you once I've heard from my contact. Or maybe he'll get in touch with you directly. Yes, that's definitely what's going to happen. I think he'll feel rejuvenated when he hears this story. I reckon you've got your hands on something precious and delicate, so make sure you don't hurt yourself—or the ones around you. It'd be a pity.

It's true that you haven't written anything yet, luckily enough—and good old Zábrana is long gone from this world. But the dead should be left in peace—all of them. Nobody's going to bring them back and it's not a good idea to meddle with certain memories. History has already been written—I hope you don't plan on trying to rewrite it."

He got up and held out his hand.

"Good-bye. I'm glad you came to see me."

THE CONTACT

It was very late when the phone rang. A light trill echoed through the room, disturbing the still of night. I was on a sofa next to the window, reading and lulled by the gentle swoosh of the river. The call startled me—it was almost as if someone from nowhere had been knocking on the door.

I picked up the receiver.

"Good evening" said a low, confident voice. "I beg your pardon for calling so late, but I wanted to be sure you'd be in. A mutual friend of ours told me about you."

"I'm surprised" I said. "Hardly anyone has this number." "Exactly—hardly anyone. And our job is to know things." "I'm sure it is. And it must be quite an interesting job."

"It is indeed. It keeps you young and alert and open to change. Because, you know, things do change. And sometimes they change to stay the same. Anyway, I see you like observing too—and you've noticed some things worthy of being investigated. Our friend gave me all the details. We can meet up, if you'd like, so we can compare notes."

"That would be great. When and where should we meet?"

"How about the day after tomorrow at four o'clock? We can meet at the Kavárna Velryba café-bar, so you feel safe. I know this is like a second home to you. And a lot of people know you—more people than you think, believe me. So bear this in mind—every move you make is out in the open."

I didn't answer.

"You're right, it's late. I don't want to waste your time. I'll be at the Kavárna Velryba the day after tomorrow. Have a pleasant night."

KAVÁRNA VELRYBA

I walked into the Kavárna Velryba half an hour ahead
of the agreed rendezvous so I could find a safe corner
where to make myself comfortable and have a clear view
of everything as I waited for the world to reveal itself
and for events to unfold. I wasn't scared and wouldn't be
taken in by appearances. Time slowed to a crawl, as did
the spiralling smoke in the light filtering in through the
windows. You could wait for nightfall forever in that
place. The afternoon stillness was almost stagnant and I
couldn't feel anything move; the secret energy of
impending encounters faded away as the minutes passed;
nothing seemed to filter in as the gears of time ground
on, driving the irreparable motion of things. I was waiting for something that wouldn't come; it was hiding,
holding back, perhaps to suggest its power and unfathomable control.

I sought solace in the habitual gestures and sounds
that secretly kept the place alive—but something kept
me down, beyond the peaceful margin of life, where
there is nothing but the emptiness of waiting.

An hour had elapsed since the meeting was scheduled;
I had finished my *turecka* so I started leafing through the

papers on the sill. And just when I was about to leave, a smart man appeared on the steps of Kavárna Velryba. He looked unfamiliar with the place; he went down a flight of stairs and looked around, as if he couldn't see the person he was meant to meet.

He was holding a pile of papers and a white envelope.

He stopped in the entrance hall leading to the tea-room, looking thoughtful. He glanced at his watch and then turned to glance at the street, hesitating all the time. He seemed anxious.

Then he moved towards the bar, zigzagging among the tables barely more than a metre from me. And at that moment he inadvertently, or so it seemed, dropped the envelope, which landed on the floor next to me.

He bent down to pick it up, dusted it off and laid it on my table. Then he glanced at me and smiled slightly, as if to excuse himself. Without a word, and still looking preoccupied, he slowly headed to the stairs. He turned for a second and then climbed the steps and left without a sound.

For an instant I couldn't quite figure out what had happened. I looked out of the window but couldn't see him. I knew then that he wouldn't be back.

I instinctively seized the envelope, which was unsealed. I opened it.

In it was a high-quality picture taken with a telescopic lens. I could see a solitary figure leaving a building; he was almost in the foreground. And there was no mistaking it—that person was me.

THE PHONE CALL

I was sure I'd get another call. And two days later I did, once again late at night.

It was the same voice, the same mock merriness and the same feigned good mood. "Good evening" he said.

"Good evening" I answered. "I see you have a lot of respect for my habits." He laughed unpleasantly and coughed.

"The other day there were still some things that needed checking out and we couldn't talk to you securely. But as you can see, we didn't leave you on your own and in fact we've shown you undivided attention."

I didn't answer. This obviously surprised him, so he tried to prod me.

"I can't say we didn't know who you are but we thought it would be wise to look into your habits—and your contacts."

"I'm flattered. Have you figured out which side I look best from? And how much sugar I put in my coffee? I'm sure you've unearthed some pretty useful stuff."

His tone revealed he had not appreciated my words. He retorted dryly:

"Maybe it's time to have you talk to someone who gets down to business. Let me point out that we have no intention of helping you or even of validating your theory. All we want to do is give our version of the events. It's in our interest that certain historical truths remain as they are and that certain essential ideas are safeguarded. All attempts to upset any of this will be met with direct consequences. But I hope you don't plan on subverting consolidated historical truths."

"I have no intention of the kind" I answered. "All I want is to investigate certain theories. And they're not theories of my own—I read about them and you can too. I've always been very perplexed about the freedom of the press. Sure, back in the day things were easier; but we can still do something now. Anyway, while you decide what to do, is there any chance of me speaking with your man?"

"I see you're anxious to hear from our sources. That's good. I can make an appointment for the day after tomorrow, at Café Slavia, in the morning. Our man isn't too keen on your college student haunts—he's more into other things."

"Good for him. It must mean he's always been on the right side. I'd appreciate it if you could refrain from making me wait around for nothing this time."

"Don't worry—it won't be a waste of time, I can assure you." "Good night."

"Good night."

A CONVERSATION AT CAFÉ SLAVIA

It was late morning and Café Slavia was almost empty. The odd tourist gazed at the selection of chocolates and pastries, breathing in the warm aroma in the hope of finding traces of a long-gone past. I gazed at the trams rolling by at the crossing—that hypnotic, eternal gliding of theirs beyond generations and men, promising endless movement along the river, the city, the outlying neighbourhoods, the future.

My contact appeared out of the blue as I was caught up in my own thoughts. He sat in front of me without a word, with the dogged silence of a man who doesn't need to ask anything.

He smiled and then whispered, "Here I am."

We'd never met and yet I could tell from his body language that he knew me and had full command over what concerned me. He asked me mockingly if I'd found anything I liked the day before at an *antikvariát* in Vinohrady.

I answered that the package I'd walked out with showed I had.

After a short silence he decided it was time to talk about the issues I'd laid out on the table—that restless, dogged past lying under the sediment of time and yet pulsing away, demanding its own light were it even in the vain present of the living.

The summer of 1980 was stifling—the heat and an air of perpetual imprisonment following Charter 77, the turns of a screw, the increasingly obsessive monitoring of everything that might be a hotbed of opposition or rebellion. With dogged resignation, Zábrana always went to his favourite cafés. He'd often spend time at the Malešice pub just outside his house, then he'd move to the town centre; he patronised Waldek in Václavské Náměstí as well as another café in Náměstí Míru; he'd even come here to the Slavia to play chess with some other patron.

Who knows—maybe he met his source here. But Václavské Náměstí is more likely. They'd meet up every now and then when the other guy came back from Moscow, took a break from his studies or repaid a favour to those who gave him so much freedom.

Zábrana's work as a translator had earned him several contacts with American scholars; in fact, we long doubted the exact identity of his sources and the actual nature of the information he received. It was always stuff having to do with literature and maybe a smattering of politics with no objective proof, but it was our job to look into every single thing.

We're pretty sure the talk took place towards the end of summer. His informer was about to come out with an important book for his own career. Maybe he was over-excited; maybe he thought the limitations of common citizens didn't apply to him and that the confidential information he owned could be passed on safely. Whatever the case, he told Zábrana about that operation, going into every detail and not bending the truth in the slightest, even though twenty years had passed. In fact, it was all so accurate that Zábrana asked him where that information came from. At this point he became hesitant—he couldn't rattle off his list of contacts and how they were connected. So he simply assured him that the source of the information was completely reliable and very close to the higher-ups who had carried out the operation.

Zábrana was deeply shocked but circumstances were on our side: his daily worries drew his focus elsewhere. It was an especially tough time in literature and politics, and the events went back twenty years so he had virtually no way of spreading the news in a credible manner.

Furthermore, the source realised he'd made a mistake opening up like that and told Zábrana it wasn't something to mess with and to keep every word of that conversation to himself, assuring Zábrana he would never admit to anything if the information leaked.

Zábrana wrote down what he'd heard in his diary and somehow ended up burying what he knew, without ever forgetting it. Maybe he was waiting for the right moment—but it would never come. The burden of his fatalism, his distrust in the present, his almost mortal certainty that nothing would change for generations led him to believe that the truth could no longer win and that the famous saying *pravda vítězí*, "truth prevails", had also been condemned by history and by something more powerful.

And in any case who would ever believe him? What proof did he have? He'd been let in on a secret by a scholar whose very freedom made him all the more suspicious and who would in any case deny those words; he couldn't prove anything. He had nothing to go on and risked terrible consequences.

No, Zábrana couldn't act then and there; everything conspired to make him even more of a fatalist and believe the truth was impossible to know, let alone to spread, and that the masters, the occupiers, were there to stay for centuries if not forever.

It was over.

It was all over and he knew it.

The café was empty again and the man had vanished quickly after a brief phone call.

He had told me: "I'll get in touch with you. Don't trust the wrong people. And don't go prying around too much—the past never dies for good. It can still come back."

In that quiet room visited by the morning light as the muffled screeching of the trams echoed throughout, I was moving through a nameless time and without any exact coordinates. The eternity of things showed itself, the river, the theatre, the road, the light, the tables, the silence; the world's spheres spun away painlessly and effortlessly; a solitary man downed his early-morning shots; slender hourglasses of light stood out; a lady crossed the threshold of habit or time ordering coffee and pastries, leafing through the newspapers as if to try her luck; I felt the gravitation of everything around me as the irony of creation scattered everyone's destiny like dust on a road.

MARIE ZÁBRANOVÁ

It was time to talk to Marie Zábranová.

We'd first met years before and just for a few minutes; little did I know that one day fate would bring us together again along with the ghost of Jan Zábrana. He would often return to the present in the lives of many, thanks to the unbreakable strength of his words, in his room besieged by the times, by power, isolated almost in a vacuum, while life carried on for everyone else and left him mere instants to complete his long, timeless testament.

We met at a crossing in the centre of Prague—it was a place I loved despite the chaos and noise, for it was always brimming with life; and even at its quietest, it always exuded a secret energy.

We recognised each other instantly. We were both fearful of the time that had past and both felt this meeting was important, that the darkness of time was converging right there, at that hour and along those very roads.

We sat in a café in the shadow of a quiet courtyard.

I had already told her over the phone why I wanted to meet and had detailed how important that passage I had retrieved from silence was. However, for a few minutes we found it hard to broach the topic—there was something extremely fragile and delicate between us, like the ashes of a lost life that refused to give in, unbreakable as it was and ready to face the future, the lives of others, the memory of those who knew, as well as the indifference of those who couldn't or didn't want to remember.

Little by little, almost as if she were pulling them out of thin air, Marie Zábranová gathered the first fragments of the past, the places, the scenes, the instants lived by Jan Zábrana when they spent their lives together.

I listened and took notes and every now and then I'd remember something. It felt as if the past were suddenly eating up the distance separating us from him and that the narrated facts and events had happened just a few days earlier. Perhaps Jan Zábrana was there, just around the corner, waiting to pop in and take a seat next to us.

Every now and then Marie would stop, her hardships of the moment evident from her breathing, her anxiety, her sudden pauses.

Only a few places from those times stood out and recurred in her recollection: the Malešice pub, the house, the places in Náměstí Míru and Václavské Náměstí, the Slavia café, where one would mince words and whisper because there could be bugs all over the place.

At the time, talking over the phone was unthinkable: everything was monitored and sometimes you could actually hear the hiss of the interception, like an open window. Some were daring enough to say hello to the unmistakable noise of the person listening in. In other cases you could tell someone was spying because the speaker's voice echoed slightly. "Just imagine" she said, "that when you called me last night I clearly heard that echo. Who knows, maybe it's going to happen again. The past never really dies."

I thought I'd already heard that sentence—from the powers that be, though.

Zábrana had led a peaceful life. Most of the time he was either writing or translating, largely from home, surrounded by books and papers, in an impregnable area that no-one—not even Marie—could enter. And in that strange, controlled disorder he always knew exactly where to find a sheet of paper, a book or a note. His papers were precious and untouchable, just like the notebooks that made up his diary, that quietly stayed with him over the years and that only towards the end of his life, when his days were numbered, were shown to Marie for what they were: Jan's silent and incessant battle against his times, against the obtuse hand of the regime that stifled his talent and his ideas and forced him into anonymity as he celebrated a handful of hopeless government servants, ministerial scribblers, pale unenlightened realists, hirelings faithful to the cultural line.

His was a lost cause but he projected his work into the future, betting everything on the unknown, on the time after him, on the new atmosphere that was bound to come eventually, like that brief moment in 1968, but this time forever.

The masters were still there but time was eroding the ground beneath their feet, and the treads of their tanks—that very time that made civilisations as well as oppression and tyranny crumble. Time had become his refuge and now time was betraying him. Time was no longer on his side. Sure, it would bring down that Iron Curtain concealing so many lives, but he wouldn't be there to see the day for which he had striven for decades.

It was a lost cause, but Marie was still there and so were the words he had dedicated to the unfailing honour he and his parents had upheld even in defeat. He hadn't followed the legion of government servants, and had paid for it. But his honour and dignity were unscathed and his tireless memory had saved, sorted and catalogued almost thirty years of his daily life and of his country's real history. Even the political masters would pass on but his diary would not: it was a crazy hope, perhaps nothing more than a delusion, but he had righteousness on his side, of those driven not by power but by the will to see when everyone else wants to forget.

He was Jan Zábrana.

He was never a government servant.

A hopeless struggle corrodes, wears out and destroys people.

His illness came on suddenly, allowing him no second chance or any extra time. Time had abandoned him.

He showed his notebooks to Marie, telling her how crucial and dangerous they were. He had been very cautious, often editing out names and descriptions, excising dates and places. But all the events were still recognisable; some names just couldn't be concealed. Many people would be in danger if those diaries ended up in the wrong hands. But with Marie they were safe: she was cut from the same cloth as him; she wouldn't give in and she wouldn't make any mistakes. Their times had also bred indestructible people who could withstand the worst.

Marie kept all Jan's papers safe and resisted quietly until the years ebbed away, gradually undermining and dispersing the state's masters and their servants. Little by little, there was room again for people to speak freely without being censored or fearing for their well-being. Jan Zábrana's time was back.

When his diaries were published, an army of people from the shadows flocked to buy them: some had long kept quiet and could now hear the voice of the lost years, the piercing words that couldn't be vocalised, the resolute judgment that didn't fear authority and lies.

When she was done, Marie looked at me as if she were momentarily scared of what she had recalled, of the immense darkness of a past that stretched away to yesteryear. But she snapped out of it right away. She sat up and once again showed that solidity, that unbreakable firmness that had enabled her to resist and defeat dreadful powers.

Suddenly, as if to focus on a more important issue, she pushed back the images of the past to tackle a central issue: who were her husband's interlocutors? As far as she could recall, only three men had access to reliable information from Moscow; all three had often travelled to and lived in the Soviet capital and would have had the right contacts to retrieve classified information.

One was a great literary historian, one was a migrated sociologist and one was a very experienced translator from Russian.

Only one of them was still alive and could still give his account. The other two could no longer speak to us.

THE SOURCES

Born Jiří Gibian, George Gibian was a Czech-American professor of Russian and comparative literature who had taught at Cornell University from 1961 to 1999. He was born in Prague in 1924 and in 1939, following the Nazi occupation, had moved to St Edmund's College in Hertfordshire, before his family left England for the United States in 1940.

After graduating from Pittsburgh University he joined the US Army in 1943, fighting with the 94th Infantry Division that landed in Normandy in 1944. He was then assigned to the Third Army of General Patton and was awarded a Bronze Star.

He studied at the Johns Hopkins University School of Advanced International Studies and earned a PhD in comparative literature at Harvard in 1951. He taught at Smith College until 1959 and at the University of California, Berkeley, till 1960. In 1961 he joined the Russian literature department of Cornell University.

He often travelled to the Soviet Union and to Eastern Europe, especially Czechoslovakia. Czech intelligence reports state that in 1974 he was in Prague to meet Milan Kundera, who would flee to Paris the following year.

He often met up with Jan Zábrana in Prague. In 1975, on his way back from Moscow, he stopped in Prague and, as Marie Zábranova recalls, he and her husband got together. They remained in touch until 1984, just before Zábrana's death.

He might have been the source of the information concerning Camus' accident, but he died at his home in Ithaca on 24 October 1999.

He'll never be able to tell us about Jan Zábrana, Prague in the Seventies and, perhaps, Albert Camus.

Jiří Zuzanek was phoned by Marie Zábranová when the Camus case went international. Professor Zuzanek said he didn't know anything about it and wasn't the one who had spoken to Jan Zábrana about the episode.

Professor Zuzanek graduated in sociology from Prague. He left Czechoslovakia in 1968 following the Soviet invasion and taught for many years at Waterloo University, where he is still professor emeritus. His most important book is *Work and Leisure in the Soviet Union: A Time-Budget Analysis*, published in 1980.

Zuzanek is fluent in Russian; he often travelled to the Soviet Union and in the years of Prague had a reputation for being very well informed on national and international matters as well as being close to circles of influence.

The third person Marie Zábranová believed might have told her husband about the Camus incident was Jiří Barbaš, an experienced translator from Russian into Czech. Unfortunately he too died a few years ago and cannot answer our questions.

Marie Zábranová recently spoke to Barbaš' wife, who claimed her husband was well acquainted with what went on in the Soviet Union and might very well have been Zábrana's source. There's no certainty, though.

Other people in his circle have told Marie Zábranová that Barbaš might have been her husband's informer, given his solid web of contacts in the Soviet Union. Marie referred to this widely held opinion in an interview with Czech national radio.

Josef Škvorecký, a renowned Czech writer who migrated to Canada and the author, in his youth, of four joint novels with Jan Zábrana, offered his opinion during a call to Marie Zábranová. He said that Zábrana was close friends with the Russian writer Vasilij Aksënov, who was also very well informed on what was going on in the Soviet Union. So he might have been Zábrana's source. Unfortunately Aksënov died in Moscow in 2009.

Time is quickly washing away most of the protagonists from that era. Fewer and fewer people are left to tell us about those years that were so pivotal for Europe's fate. And thus there will be fewer and fewer chances to find out the truth about certain crucial events.

MARIE ZÁBRANOVÁ'S STORY

I met Marie Zábranová again.

The landslide of memories frozen in time had been released and was gathering speed. All it had taken to jolt it was the attempt to remember, the summoning of ghosts that seemed gone for good, remembering acts that seemed to have been carried out in an eternal present. The past decades and the shift in the world's balance of power now enabled those suspended lives to resurface in her conscience. While there was no going back to change even a hint of the past, at last that great, unbreakable time could be told, that time that had been preserved in the memory, safe from the brunt of passing eras and the threat of Dark Ages that always seemed poised to return to cast their shadow of danger and suspicion even on the new order built on the old masters.

Marie wasn't too keen on phone calls.

She spent her life knowing someone else was listening in, whether she was at home, at work or just talking to her close friends. When you spend every day of your life under threat, it becomes hard to trust new circumstances and hope that life will give you a break or even protect you.

Recently, after the uproar caused by the publication of her husband's writings, she thought she could hear the same echo on the phone that used to mean someone was listening in. There's no way to tell for sure now but the persistence of such measures cannot be ruled out in most former Warsaw Pact countries, especially the former states of the USSR, where the veil of democracy is laughably and increasingly thin.

Marie claimed that Jan Zábrana's path crossed with that of a crucial figure in the cultural debate of the Fifties and Sixties: Boris Pasternak.

Jan Zábraná was especially fond of *Doctor Zhivago* and went out of his way to translate it into Czech. As the years went by and the political situation changed, he started to believe he could do it. It would be a long struggle, but he was sure he could win.

The fortunes of that novel and its author were also tied to Albert Camus' endeavours. He sought to use his influence to persuade the jury to select Pasternak for the Nobel Prize for Literature that he had been awarded the year before.

It is quite singular how the lives of Zábrana, Camus and Pasternak crossed: their integrity, their freedom of spirit, their common pursuit of human and artistic truth was fruitful and fatal for all here. The history of those years and Soviet power conspired in different ways to silence and annihilate them. Their fate was tragic but the fruit of their creation has stood the test of time and resisted the very power that repressed their work and decided their fates.

CAMUS AND PASTERNAK

There are two threads we can follow in Marie Zábranová's story and in the lives of these authors. One has to do with the relationship between Camus and Pasternak, who exchanged several letters; the latter eventually won the Nobel prize in 1958 as Camus grew more and more hostile to the Soviet regime. The other has to do with the almost novel-like events that enabled Jan Zábrana to translate *Doctor Zhivago* into Czech.

Albert Camus was a long-time admirer of Boris Pasternak and in his Nobel Prize acceptance speech had referred to the Russian novelist as "the great". He appreciated his work as a whole and planned on writing a play based on Pasternak's *Slepaja Krasavica* (The Blind Beauty). The uproar caused by *Doctor Zhivago* and the outrage generated in Europe by the tribulations it went through in the Soviet Union as well as the sheer power of Pasternak's narration further convinced the author's European supporters to push for him to be awarded the 1958 Nobel prize.

The book was ready in early 1956 but Pasternak was aware that it was "virtually impossible to publish" in the

Soviet Union, at least at the time. Still, he gave a copy of the manuscript to the publishing office of the magazine *Novyj Mir*, with little hope of it being accepted.

He printed a few more copies and gave them to his most trusted friends. These included Isaiah Berlin, French PhD student Jacqueline de Proyart (who eventually got permission from Pasternak to represent it abroad), and most importantly Sergio D'Angelo, who passed it on to the renowned Italian publisher Giangiacomo Feltrinelli. Feltrinelli immediately realised how monumental the book was and set to work to get an exclusive contract with Pasternak. He managed to do so even though the writer didn't want to preclude other options. Thus began a long battle to publish the book, in the teeth of Soviet opposition and to the perplexity of the Italian communists.

After a long tug-of-war and despite opposition and obstacles of all kinds, Feltrinelli achieved his goal: on 23 November 1957 the novel was published in Italy, translated by Pietro Zveteremich and titled *Il dottor Zivago*. The book immediately became a best-seller and publishers all across Europe scrambled to follow in Feltrinelli's steps. On 23 June 1958 the book was published in France by Gallimard.

On 9 June 1958 Camus, who was aware of the book's troubled publication since he was an editor at Gallimard, wrote to Pasternak expressing his great admiration and hinting at the support he was willing to give him. It was no coincidence that the letter came with a copy of his acceptance speech, where he explicitly praised Pasternak.

Discreetly but without ever concealing his opinion in public, Camus championed Pasternak's candidature for the 1958 Nobel prize and encouraged other intellectuals to support the Russian writer as well.

At the time Camus, who was already very well known and a fresh Nobel prize recipient, was probably the most influential and listened-to intellectual in the world. His stature as a righteous man always in pursuit of justice, his fight against dictatorship and his defence of the oppressed worldwide made him an exemplary figure, respected and esteemed globally. His words and opinion were of immeasurable weight; and his support of Pasternak was yet another blow to Soviet power after the clamorous and unrestrained protest he had stirred up following the invasion of Hungary.

Camus took a stand yet again, this time to hinder the Soviet efforts to stifle the outrage caused by the publication of Pasternak's book. He had become the Soviets' nemesis, the most influential and forward-thinking intellectual in Europe; he treated French communists like puppets, mobilised the disdain of public opinion against the Hungarian massacre and now fuelled the flames of a scandal that had turned from literary to political and helped to destroy any delusion of a post-1956 de-Stalinisation.

Maybe the Pasternak case really was the straw that broke the camel's back—it proved that Camus was a sworn enemy and it was time to get rid of him.

On 28 June, Pasternak replied, mentioning to Camus that his life had turned a new page, that he was inspired by Camus and grateful also for their friendship and the French writer's unwavering support in the face of adversity. He was above all fulsome in praise of Camus.

The letter was unsigned. Pasternak never signed his letters, hoping it would help him bypass censorship.

On 14 August, Pasternak wrote to Camus again, asking if he had received his first letter. Here he sounds even warmer and more brotherly, and hints that he didn't necessarily expect an answer from Camus but even just a sign or news and that he was grateful all the same.

There was very little time left to apply for the Nobel Prize and, even though it wasn't official, there was a major problem: *Doctor Zhivago* had been published in Italian and French but not in the original Russian. In the absence of a Russian edition, the Nobel board could not award the prize to Pasternak.

The race to help him win his battle had begun much earlier, though. Feltrinelli was preparing a Russian text to be published in Italy and, basing his work on the copy owned by Jacqueline de Proyart, he was progressing nicely with the help of the Dutch publisher Mouton.

Some scholars claim the Mouton edition was supported by the CIA, which would further distribute the book in October 1958 at the Brussels Expo, where several Russian copies of the book without the original frontispiece were made available.

Indeed, apparently authorised by Feltrinelli, on 24 August 1958, just in time for Pasternak's application and on the cusp of the appearance of the Italian edition, the Russian edition by Mouton became available, the first page being glued on and featuring the title of the book and the publisher's name (in Cyrillic): "G. Feltrinelli, Milan".

Pasternak's application had been saved and Soviet irritation grew further, since the Russian text could now reach the nomenclatura, or party apparatus, as well as intellectuals and all those who could travel abroad.

It seems that the CIA's supposed involvement with the Mouton publication had to do with the text's typesetting, which was carried out in collaboration with a non-official section of the CIA in Europe, the CUPE (Central Union of Post-war Emigres).

There are different versions about how the CIA got its hands on the text. One mentions an unscheduled stop-over of a flight in Malta, where CIA agents made a copy of the book found in a suitcase, without the owner noticing. In fact, it is likely that several copies made it to the West where the American or British intelligence agencies could easily have obtained one.

Shortly after the Mouton edition came out, Feltrinelli also published a Russian version that was long available in Italy and, as we shall see, eventually made its way into Jan Zábrana's hands.

On 23 October 1958, the efforts of Camus, Feltrinelli and of all those who had believed in his book came to fruition as Boris Pasternak was awarded the Nobel Prize, which triggered an extreme reaction within the USSR.

Failing to realise that the brutality of the crackdown would damage their image far more than any novel ever would—and *Doctor Zhivago* was not even anti-Soviet—Moscow's official reaction unforgivingly reproduced the traditional Stalinist playbook.

On 26 October, *Literaturnaya Gazeta* published a scathing article by the prominent Soviet journalist and propagandist David Zaslavsky. Students on humanities courses were encouraged to sign a petition against Pasternak and his novel. A "spontaneous rally" was then organised for them to demand that the writer be exiled from the Soviet Union. On 29 October, at the central committee of the League of Young Communists, on the occasion of the Komsomol's fortieth anniversary, Vladimir Semichastny, who headed the KGB from 1961 onwards, attacked Pasternak in a speech, calling him a pig. Khrushchev looked on and applauded along with thousands of other people. It is believed that the most offensive passages of his speech were fed to him by Khrushchev, who loved subverting traditional forms of communication, often veering into vulgarity.

Pasternak was assured that if he went to Stockholm to accept the award he would never be allowed to come back to Russia. Threats were also made to his beloved Olga Ivinskaya, who due to her bond with Pasternak had already spent four years in a labour camp under Stalin and had lost the baby she carried when she was arrested.

This was almost too much to bear for Pasternak and he even contemplated taking his own life.

After some anguished days in which his wife and loved ones tried to convince him to give up the Nobel prize, a shattered Pasternak sent a second wire to Stockholm, this time telling the Committee that he had to decline the award due to the impact it would have on the society in which he lived.

In the following days, despite his step back, Pasternak still suffered persecution. The Writers' Union assailed him in the press and on 31 October a closed-door trial was held to decide on Pasternak's banishment. Furthermore, a petition at the Politburo was set in place to revoke his citizenship and exile him to the West.

Pasternak was devastated. His health was seriously compromised. In fact, it is likely that the seeds of his final illness had been sown.

In January 1960, just a few months before dying, the writer Olga Andreyeva Carlisle met him in his dacha.

It was probably one of Pasternak's last exchanges with someone from the West.

The novelist told him that Camus had died in a car crash just a few days earlier. Pasternak was grief-stricken.

He hadn't heard anything about the accident.

Camus' works weren't translated in the Soviet Union and the media had ignored news of the crash.

As far as the Soviet powers were concerned, Camus no longer existed.

Boris Pasternak died late on 30 May 1960, apparently because of lung cancer and shortly after the death of the man who, appropriately enough, had been the closest to him in his final years.

Rescuers take a last look at the shattered wreck of the custom built Facel Vega car in which Albert Camus and Michel Gallimard were travelling.

Albert Camus's coffin being carried from Villeblevin Town Hall on the way to internment at Lourmarin in the Vaucluse, 5 January 1960.

Albert Camus receives the Nobel Prize for Literature.

Albert Camus signing copies of *The Rebel* with a wrapper announcing he had won the Nobel Prize for Literature.

Imre Nagy, Prime Minister of Premier of Hungary during the 1956 Revolt against the Soviets.

Dmitri Shepilov, former Minister of Foreign Affairs of the Soviet Union.

Albert Camus (1913–1960).

Boris Leonidovich Pasternak, 1890–1960, Russian novelist and admirer of Camus.

Albert Camus (1913–1960).

Plaques in Villeblevin commemorating the death of Camus.

IN PURSUIT OF *DOCTOR ZHIVAGO*

Marie Zábranová is a strict, sometimes even severe person. Her sharp, unflinching gaze seems to be looking for the truth and the sense of past and present in things. Her memory is a steel trap, with time and events crystallised therein as if she had to save them for the future, for a moment in which history could really judge the living and the dead with fairness.

Remembering is sometimes painful to her; you can tell it from her face even though her expression is always composed and her voice firm. When she has happy she beams, showing how hope and generosity have never left her despite the sometimes tragic hardships she has had to face.

She speaks warmly about how entranced her husband Jan was after reading just a part of *Doctor Zhivago*. He wanted to translate it into Czech but had no idea of the hardships he and Marie would have to endure for the sake of that book.

In 1963 Zábrana had managed to get a microfilm of the Russian text, but it was very hard to make out. So he had begun, out of sheer enjoyment, to translate a part of it, without really thinking about getting it published. He had translated the chapters "Varykino" and "Epilogue", the easiest to make out on the microfilm. He was hoping to get his hands on the complete Russian text, which was nowhere to be found in Czechoslovakia.

At long last, in spring 1965 that long-awaited glimmer of hope came. His wife Marie, who was an editor at the Odeon and of the magazine *Světova Literatura*, was invited along with all the editorial staff to take part in a cultural trip to Italy. The participants included art historian Jaromír Neumann, artist Adolf Born and Odeon editor-in-chief Jan Řezáč. The delegation from Odeon, the main Czech publishing house, would travel by bus to a number of northern Italian places of artistic interest, going as far as Florence.

It would be a once-in-a-lifetime chance to buy the Russian text of *Doctor Zhivago* published in Italy by Feltrinelli. It would also be a chance to meet Fernanda Pivano, whom she often wrote to. Allen Ginsberg had stayed with the Zábranas in Prague and had written Pivano a letter to introduce her to his Czech friends. Ginsberg was among the authors translated by Zábrana and, after visiting Prague and consolidating his friendship with Jan, was unfortunately expelled from the country. He casually told the policemen escorting him to the border that he owed Mr Zábrana some money and asked if he could give it to him.

In late April 1965, Marie, who had given birth to little Eva in October 1964, left for Italy bearing a huge responsibility and knowing she'd have to take some risks. The group was accompanied by an interpreter guide, who had clearly been tasked with monitoring their every move and reporting any improper behaviour to the authorities. Furthermore, there was no way to be sure all the travellers could be trusted; indeed, Marie suspected there might be other potential informers among them.

Any move she made on behalf of her husband would have to be carried out on her own, away from all the other travellers.

In the centre of Milan she managed to meet Fernanda Pivano, who at the time lived in Via Manzoni. She told her about her husband's plan to translate *Doctor Zhivago*. Pivano had a good relationship with Feltrinelli and would certainly act as a go-between so that the rights to the book could go to Czechoslovakia as well. It was a warm and fruitful meeting and both agreed on how important it was to get the novel published in as many countries as possible.

In Venice, Marie met Sergio Molinari, an Italian professor of Russian literature who was also teaching at the University of Prague and with whom the Zábranas were friends. They met close to Piazza San Marco and spent some forty minutes chatting on a bench. But someone saw them and two months later, Marie was called in by the secret police and drilled about the meeting. They said that Molinari was believed to be a spy and a treacherous man. Marie retorted by telling them he often stayed at their place in Prague and was the farthest thing from a spy or secret agent. Given her obvious peace of mind, they let her go with no further consequences.

When they arrived in Florence, Marie carried out the first part of her plan.

She had brought along a golden brooch given to her by Jan when their daughter was born. She went to a jeweller close to Ponte Vecchio and traded in the brooch, which she had to relinquish to get the book. It was a tough decision and a sad moment—but Jan's wish for *Doctor Zhivago* was more important. In exchange for that beloved object she got precious Italian currency that she could use to buy the book, which Marie eventually found in Bologna.

She could hardly believe she was holding the volume she and her husband had been after for so many years. She hid it among other harmless books in her bag.

Soon they would be heading home but her joy at achieving her objective was tempered by fear. *Doctor Zhivago* was forbidden in the Soviet Union and customs checks were bound to be exacting. Jan had warned her there might be consequences. Then Marie had an idea. Seeing all her colleagues buying souvenirs, she too decided to make a purchase: with what money she had left she bought a pram for her daughter in Prague. The pram would be her Trojan horse.

At the border, customs officers boarded the Odeon bus to investigate the passengers' luggage. They hardly even glanced at the books but thoroughly searched the pram. After examining it from top to bottom, they left. The book was safe.

At long last, Jan could read the whole novel and set to work translating it.

They got in touch with Feltrinelli through the publishing house Československý Spisovatel to obtain the rights, thanks also to the invaluable assistance of Fernanda Pivano.

By May 1967 they knew for sure that the novel would be published.

Times were changing and Czechoslovakia's political situation wasn't entirely dismal; government control and censorship were loosening up. Little did anyone expect that fateful 1968, so full of joy, freedom and hope, where everything seemed possible.

Despite the more relaxed climate, Jan was plagued by foreboding and tried to speed up the translation. He acted as if he had a deadline, as if every day dark omens drew closer. His tension was sometimes palpable, almost as if something told him fate wasn't on his side.

By the end of 1967 he had translated two thirds of the book. On 1 April 1968, in the middle of the Prague Spring, he signed a contract with the publisher. Jan had just about completed his first draft of the translation but was pleased only with part of it, so he set to work on revising his own translation.

In the summer of '68 it seemed freedom had prevailed again. The people of Prague lived their merry illusion with indescribable enthusiasm. Jan could sense danger, though, and didn't trust the ruling class, not even the men who had made the Prague Spring happen.

His premonitions were confirmed. On the night of 20 August 1968 Soviet troops, with the help of forces of the "brother" countries of the Warsaw Pact, invaded Czechoslovakia.

Even though he had never bought into the febrile atmosphere of the last few months, Jan was devastated. As had often happened in his life, all he could do was expect the worst. When Dubček returned from his "captivity" in Moscow and spoke to the nation, it was obvious that he was still a virtual prisoner. His voice was broken and he struggled to find the right words; for the whole country it was proof that the time for dreaming was over and that a new, even stricter imprisonment would crush the country.

All those who had taken advantage of the Prague Spring to speak out, express their ideas and criticise what didn't work suddenly fell silent and had no opinions, as in the Gottwald era. The regime's standard language, the tired phrases everyone mocked during the Prague Spring, was back in full spate. Questions remained unanswered; nobody had an opinion; jurisdiction always lay elsewhere; established phrases from the past proliferated once again. Minds and tongues had iced over as in the harshest years and any hope for the future had disappeared from the horizon of existence.

Jan Zábrana was well acquainted with that atmosphere. But for the books he loved, time was once again running short.

In spring 1968, some passages of *Doctor Zhivago* translated by Zábrana were published in the magazine *My68*.

The havoc following the invasion caused all projects to be put on hold. Nobody had any idea how things would develop; it wasn't known whether, once the dust settled, the Czechs would be allowed a degree of autonomy and some of the freedoms erased just a few months earlier.

The invaders felt that the country, now under military control, could not retaliate. The people, however, were restless, so in order to prevent any resounding protests the Soviets slowly restored the situation as it was before Dubček's appointment. For a few months, then, a modicum of autonomy was still possible. Amazingly, in the November–December 1968 edition of *Světova Literatura*, two chapters of *Doctor Zhivago* were published, along with Mikuláš Medek's illustrations.

With what little strength he had left and despite his shattered morale, on 16 December 1968 Jan Zábrana was able to give the publisher his completed translation. He wasn't quite satisfied with his work and would have liked to tweak it here and there, as any poet would, but he was exhausted and under intense pressure. He realised that time was against him with uncertainty and threats always looming. The way he always saw things coming was uncanny and disturbing.

Amid the general euphoria he had been the only one who couldn't celebrate, almost as if some subtle awareness warned him of the impending threats and the future tragedy. Now he knew he was right. And he knew he was right about the future, about the broken hopes, about the abyss that lay ahead.

Now, even mere survival would be an achievement. He silently waited for the cruel mechanism of history to dig in its claws, sink its iron teeth into the delicate flesh of that unlucky country. New boots worn by new barbaric masters were trampling that civilisation, that beauty, that defenceless wonder.

The months went by and nothing moved. Every act, every decision that seemed to contribute to the Prague Spring was suddenly suspended, paralysed and eventually derailed.

Everyone waited silently for the worst; and slowly, inexorably, bureaucratically, it happened. The grip the military had exerted over critical areas since 20 August 1968 was tightening, cynically stifling even the mildest initiatives.

On 11 May 1970, Jan Zábrana, like many other writers and translators, received a letter from his publisher:

"The Publishing House has changed the political and cultural direction of its publishing activities. All existing contracts have been examined to assess their correspondence with the new endeavours of the Publishing House. Consequently, the decision has been made not to publish your work."

That circular was as good as a gravestone. Years of work and the passion of those who believed in the project had been sacrificed in the name of a publishing policy and of the new caste of servants who had established themselves everywhere to take new orders from new masters.

As soon as the Soviets arrived, lists of proscribed writers and their books were drawn up: professors, lecturers, teachers, senior officials, politicians and intellectuals would soon end up working as porters, woodsmen, miners, drivers and dustmen. Important published books would be pulped; texts that bore witness to the previous era would be blocked and suppressed. No-one knew in which direction to turn; only works not to be published and ideas not to be spread were pursued with any effort.

After years of darkness, fate had given Jan a glimmer of hope and freedom. He had embraced it fully, giving it his all. But now bad luck was dimming that glint of light forever—just as he was about to complete his work.

It was over. And he knew it.

Jan Zábrana never saw the publication of his translation of *Doctor Zhivago*.

The Soviet grip on Czechoslovakia would persist for another twenty years. Jan couldn't resist that long. Overcome by bitterness, pain, the defeat of a whole generation, the eternal triumph of the mediocre and of the worst sorts, he died of liver cancer on 3 September 1984. He just had time to leave his beloved, dearest and unswerving Marie his poems, translations and, most importantly, the repository of his memories, the secret notebooks of the diary he had kept for thirty years, where future generations would recognise the past, the righteous and the traitors, those who had served and who had carried their pain with dignity and their dignity without shame.

Jan was gone but not his memory; it was all the more precious, for everything that had been wouldn't be in vain and oblivion would not confuse killers for victims, mercenaries for dreamers, informers for the vanquished.

Marie embraced the gift and committed herself to pursuing that silent fight Jan had to relinquish. Those diaries and poems were in good hands; it was just a matter of time now before history remembered that small, precious country invaded not once but twice throughout the twentieth century by its two most powerful and brutal neighbours.

History remembered Czechoslovakia.

The unstoppable decline of the invading empire led to the Velvet Revolution in 1989. Jan Zábrana's times were back.

In 1990, Marie Zábranová, with the precious help of Jaroslava Dientsbierová, finally managed to get her husband's translation of *Doctor Zhivago* published, by Lidové Nakladatelství. The long journey of that fateful book had come to an end.

Its success was immediate and exceeded expectations. An estimated 100,000 copies of the first edition were sold—a rare event for a quality book. A second edition was printed in 2003 and included among the classics of Euromedia Group Odeon; a third edition was printed in 2005 for Lidové Noviny. At last, Czech readers could also read the book that had been condemned and pursued for years by an obtuse power.

In 1992, Jan Zábrana's diary was also published with the title *Celý život* (A Whole Life): 1,100 pages of history, the daily life of Czechoslovakia in its glacial years. It was yet another gift from Jan to those who, like him, had never surrendered and to those who, after him, needed to know.

Marie had fulfilled her task.

Jan's memory would survive.

SUSPICION

The phone rang at about 10 p.m.

It was my first interlocutor, the man for all seasons. "Good evening" he said. "How are you?"

"I'm doing pretty well, thank you" I answered. "Your contacts haven't helped me much." "Maybe they couldn't do any more. Or maybe it wouldn't have been fair to put words into other people's mouths."

"I see. And I see you haven't forgotten about me."

"Of course not. You're a smart, hard-working person. Have you carried on with your investigation, even without any further information from us?"

"Not yet. I'm trying to make light of certain things. But time flies—everything fades away and disappears in a flash."

"Dead men tell no tales and the living would rather forget. Fear is stronger than the truth. Haven't you realised it yet?"

"Sure, fear and ulterior motives are often stronger. But the truth's strength is oblique and unpredictable. It can come from the last places or people you'd imagine and for mysterious reasons, too. Or perhaps I'm waiting for something of the kind to happen or for overlooked or disappeared proof to reappear. Anything's possible."

"I can understand your doggedness. But I doubt certain things can reappear. It wouldn't benefit any-one. That's important. You know what? I've got an opinion, considering the elements you've given me and considering the whole situation. I'm sure that if things really went the way you suspect and someone planned the whole accident, then I find it highly unlikely the local services didn't know anything about it. It might seem strange, and yet these operations always rely on cover-ups—authorisations, if you will. You see, the person in question was a troublesome intellectual and caused embarrassment to virtually all the political fac-tions. He was a party spoiler, a skilled man who knew how to pull the public opinion's strings. He irritated a lot of people—even domestically. And when you irri-tate a lot of people no-one's going to come to your rescue when you need it. No-one's going to see if something happens. Maybe that's how it went—when some outer force came to do its job, it was given the scope it needed. Blind eyes were turned. That's how things work. You know but you don't act because it's to everyone's benefit.

Are you aware of any proper, thorough investiga-tions into the crash? Or was the superficial evidence deemed enough to close the case? Car crashes work well in situations like this. Remember what happened in Bulgaria in 1973? The secret services tried to kill the Italian Communist Party secretary Enrico Berlinguer with the most mundane sort of road accident—a lorry spins out of control and crashes into the car in which the target is sitting. Sure, things were different there and the ones pulling the strings had full control over the area. Everyone on the Italian delegation realised it was intentional, and yet the lorry driver vanished right away and no investigation was carried out. The same thing happened with Camus—no-one really wanted to find out what happened. I'm not pointing any fingers but there are parallels that make me smell a rat. The absurd fate, the car crash, the seemingly inexplicable cause, on a straight road in full daylight and no proper investigation…

You'll realise it too if you try to spread this story. You'll run into a lot of trouble, first of all because you're a foreigner—certain topics are internal affairs exclusively. And then bringing up facts that have been officially ascertained is bound to ruffle some feathers. It's better to make do with the convenient official version that has been corroborated by time, by custom, by suitability. You won't have it easy, I can assure you. But I don't want to burst your bubble. After all, something always does reappear. Sometimes bodies rise to the surface; the net of reality loosens up; the past re-emerges in places and at times that nobody would expect. So don't worry—maybe you're right and something *will* pop up to validate your theory. Just try not to bother the people who could harm you. As you know, life is full of little, unexpected and potentially fatal accidents. And sometimes they seem to happen to the right people—ever wonder why? You know it all too well. So don't take too much advantage of your independence.

If you find something, I'd appreciate it if you'd let me know. Good-bye for now and don't worry about the past—it's the present we've got to look out for."

THE TRUTH ABOUT THE NAGY AFFAIR

On 16 June 1958, the Hungarian Prime Minister Imre Nagy, who had long opposed the Soviets in his struggle for Hungarian independence, was hanged with General Pál Maléter and the journalist Miklós Gimes after a show trial directed and decided by Moscow.

Powerless indignation swept over the world. In France, a group of editors studied the so-called facts, papers and evidence to prove that Imre Nagy had been "legally" killed.

A book called *The Truth about the Nagy Affair* was published in the hope of restoring the truth. Camus wrote a memorable foreword, sparing no venom for the killers and invaders of Hungary.

The foreword was also published in issue 20 of the libertarian magazine *Témoins*.

A PACIFIC LIBERTARIAN

Camus and his writing elicited a wide range of responses, and in his book published in 2012, *L'Ordre Libertaire: La Vie Philosophique d'Albert Camus*, the French philosopher and writer Michel Onfray carefully examined his thought and work. Remember that in 1951, when *The Rebel* was published, Camus' writing was slammed by Jean-Paul Sartre and his fellow, largely Stalinist, members of France's *intelligentsia*.

Time would redeem Camus' memory, as Onfray pointed out, given his unquestionable honesty, sagacity and valour. On the other hand, Sartre's cynicism, baseness and lust for personal gain masked as cultural interest have long been dismissed as a grave disappointment.

It is crystal-clear, though, that the public's view of Camus has long been tarnished by Sartre's hostility, and by his proselytes' and followers' constant efforts to besmirch Camus' work and personality.

It was a careless—or, rather, partial—reading of Camus' work and engagement that earned him a reputation as a lame Social Democrat: his only crime was his unwillingness to be as extreme and maximalist upon

certain matters as would please the wannabe revolution-
aries of Saint-Germain and the media, forever hungry
for bombastic stances.

In fact, Camus was always much closer to the libertarian and anarchist press and publications, with which he
collaborated closely. It was his true milieu of choice: he
wrote for *La Révolution prolétarienne* and for *Témoins*.

La Révolution prolétarienne fell in line with revolutionary
unionism; its manifesto, almost quoting the First International, read: "The emancipation of the working class
shall be pursued by no-one but the working class".

In his youth Camus was a member of the Communist
party: he had joined it in Algeria, in autumn 1935, but
in 1937 he was expelled because of his independent
mindset and his ideas, which were regarded as Muslim-
nationalist—and were thus incompatible with the Party's
new line.

The Algerian communist party was then under the
sway of its French sibling. When the French Popular
Front collapsed in 1938, the directives from Moscow
prompted the PCF to abruptly change course: in order
not to weaken France, the party toned down its anti-
colonialist and antimilitarist orientation.

The same abrupt change of stance was forced upon
the PCA, and precipitated intense turmoil among its
militants. It also resulted in the splitting of the Étoile
Nord-Africaine (ENA)—the Muslim Front of the Communist party. This break-away generated an extremely
thorny environment and ultimately led former brothers-
in-arms to fight each other.

In fact, just like many other left-wing youths of his
day, Camus had joined the party mostly to resist the

Fascist threat. Nonetheless, he wasn't a Marxist and nor was he very knowledgeable about Marx's works.

His intellectual freedom, his understanding of the Muslims' claims, his honesty and his loyalty to his former ENA cadres—in striking contrast to the PCA's two-facedness—cost him his membership.

We might call Camus a pacific libertarian, an enlightened anarchist. He was certainly close to some practical, libertarian socialism that strove to help the working class. He was some sort of revolutionary unionist—rather like Fernand Pelloutier, who in 1895 was already advocating the affinity between trade unionism and anarchism.

Camus' worldview, Onfray said, was rooted in the best vital motives, in a sane idea of society, in unselfish individualism, in the Mediterranean light. He couldn't be any further from the Russian Bolshevists and nihilists, from the Slavic terrorists, from Hegelian-inspired ideas, and from any delusional totalitarian grandeur.

According to Onfray, in Camus' perspective Tipaza was opposite to Berlin, Plotinus to Sade, Proudhon to Marx, Pelloutier to Lenin, and the Paris Commune to the Siberian Gulag.

He saw anarchism as an ethical thirst for real, practical social justice; a man-sized, positive anarchy.

His soul was noble and his gaze upon reality just. Thus he would never allow any bloody, barbaric means to justify humane ends. His revolt was a revolt for life; his untamed gaze brought to mind Étienne de La Boétie, who wrote: "Be determined to never serve again, and you will find that you are free".

Let us remember that the notion of the "revolt" in Camus' work is twofold. It is a metaphysical revolt against the human condition, tortured by evil and pain; but it is also a political revolt against God and men. It is a relentless, unending, necessary revolt.

According to Onfray's studies, which were partly based on Marin Progreso's 1967 book *La pensée politique d'Albert Camus*, it seems that in the early 1950s Camus approved of the manifesto of libertarian socialism written by Gaston Leval (with whom he had a minor quarrel, promptly settled, when *The Rebel* was published).

As a matter of fact, Leval's pamphlet was found amidst Camus' private papers, and it seems, in spirit, in agreement with Camus' well-known perspective. It encouraged one to cherish a libertarian ethic and, quite unlike what the Marxists preached, it eschewed the supremacy of the economy and the creation of a new man through changed means of production. On the contrary, it was a new man that was bound to change them. Revolution must be moral rather than economic, and a renewed mankind with new values would learn how to evenly distribute wealth.

Those who intend to create a new society must be morally superior to those they seek to vanquish: on this point in particular we can feel Camus' spiritual approval.

In a world which is unprincipled we can only appeal to such values as justice, brotherhood, honesty, loyalty, righteousness, dignity, sympathy and selflessness.

With its extreme materialism and distrust of the human conscience, Marxism would damage Socialism forever.

We can hear the echo of the ancient moral precepts that have always been to the fore in Camus' fight for a just society and for ethical, rather than economic, human growth.

Onfray also pointed out the affinity between Camus and Gramsci, who thought that every social revolution should first and foremost pursue a revolution in consciousness. Ideas and knowledge must pave the way for social revolution, which can take place only after a dramatic cultural change has occurred.

It is also worth underlining the proximity of Camus' thinking to Simone Weil's. Camus thought very highly of her: as an editor at Gallimard he edited seven works of Weil's (including *The Need for Roots, La condition ouvrière, Oppression and Liberty* and *Écrits de Londres)*. He also edited her *Écrits historiques et politiques*, which was published by Gallimard in March 1960, shortly after Camus' death.

Roger Quillot wrote that "Camus was fond of Simone Weil, and her work undoubtedly drew him closer to revolutionary unionism. It was a political environment very familiar to her, and in it Camus recognized her own fiery intransigence".

Lou Marin also shed light upon this libertarian Camus. He pointed out that Camus owed much to Simone Weil, and that he deeply admired her because she had willingly sacrificed her whole private life for the sake of the libertarian movement.

Camus wrote that Weil never strove for anything personal.

They were both tormented by the very same thirst for justice and truth—a thirst that would not be quenched by personal profit.

Marin also pointed out how Camus was influenced by his close acquaintance with the French anarchist Rirette Maîtrejean. They had met in Paris and, in 1940, they fled from the German invasion in the same car. In Clermont-Ferrand they would meet up almost daily for three months; later that year, in Lyon, they would see each other less frequently. Maîtrejean would later say: "We were always together".

It was she who introduced Camus to the long and bitter struggle to free Victor Serge from the Soviet gulag; and it was she who told him all about the gory show trials of the Stalin era.

There was a remarkable generational gap between the two of them—Maîtrejean was fifty-three, Camus was twenty-seven—and it's hard to tell whether it was she who lured Camus into the anarchist cause, and how. What is beyond doubt, though, is that this charismatic woman helped young Albert to develop a libertarian perspective.

Camus would untiringly object to injustice and oppression; he sided against the Spanish Fascist dictatorship and the Soviet invasion of Hungary; he was a committed philanthropist, and all this gave him a certain quixotic aura. It is no wonder that Cervantes' chivalrous, nostalgic knight was one of Camus' role models: on 23 October 1955, at the Sorbonne, he delivered a celebratory speech for the 350th anniversary of the publication of *Don Quixote*. The text was published the following November in *Le Monde Libertaire* bearing the title "Spain and Quixotry".

Honour, freedom, the defence of the weak, abused or persecuted; a mixture of generosity and a rebellion against all forms of injustice: these qualities made Don Quixote the perfect comrade for Camus. After all, they both were tireless warriors, fighting against all the odds; and never giving up in confronting the inequity—either social or metaphysical—that haunts our world.

A VALEDICTION

ALBERT CAMUS HAS DIED

The years seem not to weigh on Camus' memory. His voice is still loud and resonant; his words are immortal, just like the values he fought—and, perhaps, died—for.

And yet, how many times have we been in desperate need of his words—how many times has not only France but the whole world missed his valued, irreplaceable voice over recent decades?

Things would have gone very differently had Camus been around in 1968. Both the rebellious youth and the powers that be would have been forced to deal with his firm words, his piercing glance.

How different would François Mitterrand's left-wing victory have been in 1981; how towering a conscience would have been there to guide him through his term; how adamant a judgement would have shunned all easy compromise, all supine lenience.

A silent era went by for want of Camus' voice. Italy experienced a similar void when Pasolini died, leaving his country to be preyed upon by political patronage— a victim of flawed sovereignty, Mammon, and media control.

The empire of the media has grown enormously since Camus' death—an unsettling trend that only worsened with the advent of the internet. People have been overwhelmed by a flood of information, with no guarantee of its quality or reliability.

In this downpour of unverified news, who are we supposed to trust? Who should we turn to with our doubts and questions?

Ideologies are on the wane; faith gives no solid answers about the nature of Evil, whose power expands beyond our life-spans and beyond history itself. All intellectuals are concerned about today is how many copies of their books they sell; the only whistle-blowing they ever do is to call for help if a fire breaks out.

But men like Camus and Pasolini were of a better kind; they were far-sighted and morally superior, and therefore could pass judgement on their times. They were allowed to suggest a course of action, to stand up for principles, to remind us what the essential pillars of society are. They took it upon themselves to be the fearless discoverers of the secret abuses of power and to give voice to the weak, the exploited, the defeated.

When they passed away we all felt more alone, while the powers that be restored their unbounded dominance and undisturbed authority.

If they were here to fight with us in the name of knowledge and reason, perhaps today's intellectuals wouldn't be in such a sorry state, and their influence upon society and public opinion wouldn't be as paltry as it is.

Wars driven by imperial impulses still rage on worldwide. They are sparked off by convenience rather than by the general will, and they wear the mask of the noblest values and the cloth of the most sacred humane causes. Thinkers justify wars, and oil and infrastructure companies and arms manufacturing lobbies sponsor them.

Reality is increasingly cold and indifferent, power and profit being the only banners to fight for, bare and stripped of their original raison d'être.

Albert Camus taught us how to stand our ground.

He looked Medusa—the twentieth-century arch-enemy, Nazism—right in the eye, and Nazism was defeated.

Today's enemies are more cynical and more subtle than then, but Camus' words can still guide us through the darkness. They can still support us and keep us from losing our common sense and our freedom.

There's still hope. Before the waves of time lay waste to the frail traces of what happened from 15 March 1957 (the day of Camus' fatal speech at the Salle Wagram) to the car crash on 4 January 1960, we can still hope that some proof arises—a piece of evidence, a voice finally telling us what happened in those dark, mysterious last days.

Who knows? Perhaps this book will be the spark that lights up the hearth of truth? We owe it to Albert Camus and to his memory.

Pravda vítězí (Truth prevails).

APPENDIX

THE REVELATIONS OF JACQUES VERGÈS
AND OTHERS

Giuliano Spazzali and Jacques Vergès

The book you have just finished reading was presented by journalist Antonella Fiori at the Centofiori bookshop in Milan on 14 May 2014. Among the audience was a prominent figure: the outstanding Italian barrister and one of the leading men in the *Mani Pulite* corruption trial, Giuliano Spazzali. After the presentation, Spazzali asked to share the remarkable story of his own acquaintance with the renowned French lawyer Jacques Vergès. A committed communist right from the outset, Vergès always stood out in French courthouses ever since his defence of a group of women FLN fighters during the Algerian liberation war. It was Vergès who saved Djamila Bouhired, a resistance fighter who would eventually become his wife, from almost certain capital punishment. To save her, he pointed a finger at the whole repressive system of the French army, deployed in Algeria in a desperate attempt to crush its quest for independence. The actions of Vergès, however, nearly cost him his own life: he was in the sights of *La Main Rouge*—the French intelligence organisation whose goal was to assassinate the lawyers working for the National Liberation Front living in Paris. It was *La Main Rouge* that executed Amokrane Ould Aoudia by shotgun on 21 May 1959. Vergès was next on *La Main Rouge's* death list, and he was spared only thanks to the mediation of General Paul Grossin, the head of the **SDECE** (External Documentation and Counter-Espionage Service).

In the late '60s, Spazzali went to France in connection with several trials of Italian political fugitives. On this occasion he made friends with Vergès—a friendship born out of personal and professional amity.

Their acquaintance lasted for years and Spazzali had the chance to listen to Vergès' own account of Camus' death.

Vergès was absolutely confident in what he said and stressed how the version of events he was giving, rather than merely a partial opinion, was the outcome of hard facts he knew of. He said that Camus' fatal accident had been painstakingly staged by a KGB section and tamely acquiesced to by French intelligence. Spazzali sent me a handwritten account to corroborate his story:

This is what I remember of the story Vergès told me. I met him—a well-famed lawyer, renowned for his revolutionary defence of the N. L. F. activists back in the days of the Algerian war—when he had just taken up practising law again in Paris, having just come out of a long "retirement". I met him several times in the late Sixties, and every time it was a remarkable meeting. Vergès and I would often meet for reasons not related to work. At the time France was brimming with Italian political "fugitives"—either sentenced or waiting for a verdict—so we had many requests for extradition to deal with. However, we would often wander away from business—a rather natural tendency for those who happen to have other interests than criminal law. It was during one of these digressions with my distinguished friend that he hinted at—or rather, firmly stated—his own idea about the circumstances of Camus' death. Vergès was convinced that the writer didn't die in a common car accident; in fact, he said that the accident had been staged.

It is my opinion that Vergès had more evidence than he cared to share with me; I, on the other hand, refrained from asking. Discretion is the best attitude when a hot topic rises unexpectedly. I didn't investigate any further, and yet I remember how Vergès was certain that the staged accident was schemed by a KGB section with the endorsement of the French intelligence.

Vergès was close to the most secret business of the powers that be. He was especially close to the communists, who had been supporting the NKVD's and the GPU's moves in France. The Soviets' moves included countless abductions and executions of both opponents and fugitives.

His account is extremely important and it dovetails with the statements of many contemporaries of Camus'. Several witnesses remember how, after having published *The Rebel* (*L'Homme révolté*, 1951) and after his falling-out with Sartre, Camus had been constantly attacked by the communist party and by parts of the French left wing, who labelled him a "fascist" and publicly boycotted him. This attitude was revealed in a letter written by Louis Aragon, as well as in the press affiliated to the PCF.

The Soviets loathed Camus and he was publicly frowned on by the PCF, which at the time actively cooperated with the KGB, especially in regards to undercover actions. In the post-war years, particularly from the late Fifties, France had been closely scrutinised by Soviet intelligence, whose aim was to exploit the French-Russian amity that came into existence after WW2. This led to growing Soviet influence in French politics, as well as to major espionage networks penetrating the highest ranks of power. The final result of this trend was the definitive break-off of France from the United States and from the rest of Europe—a split that would eventually translate into De Gaulle's decision to leave NATO in 1966. In hindsight, these events can be regarded as a massive investment in France—a fruitful investment, which fed upon France's innate wariness of the United States, regarded as historical and cultural reckless colonisers. It was an impressive political operation and it left behind a huge trail of written evidence, not limited to history books but also in the newspapers, which over the years gave accounts of the scandals and undercover activities perpetrated in France by Soviet intelligence.

Albert Camus was killed for a very precise reason: he interfered with the coalition between the USSR and France. He was a strenuous opponent of the Soviet invasion of Hungary, and he was a person of international prominence: by overtly disassociating himself from Sartre and from the French communist party, Camus ended up being an obstacle to the—not necessarily transparent—political processes of cooperation between Paris and Moscow. Camus' prominent character, with his well-known anti-Soviet attitude, stood out in the eyes of the French people as a reminder of the USSR's cruel imperialism. Both the French and the Soviet government would have benefited greatly from silencing this unpleasant nuisance. Perhaps reason of state turned a blind eye on the conspiracy of silence: a long-arranged plan was carried out at last, and Camus was killed. His car crash was regarded as a mere accident and no proper investigation was carried out. After his death, he was put on an idealised pedestal from where he could do no harm. There, amidst France's wisest sages, his sharp critical judgment was ineffective. Sartre and the PCF hastened Camus' *damnatio memoriae*. The Soviet spies, infiltrated at every level in the hierarchy of French society, were at last free to pursue their objectives and reach their goals.

It is important to bear in mind that Jacques Vergès, who had no doubt that the KGB was involved in the Camus incident, had been the general secretary of the International Union of Students from 1951 to 1954. The Union had been founded in Prague in 1946. In this front organisation, which was controlled by the Soviet Union, he worked closely with its vice-president and his friend Aleksandr Šelepin, the man who later ran the KGB at the time of Camus' death. The International Union of Students recruited cadres for many European communist parties, often obtained their affiliation to the KGB, and in later years its elderly members were always connected by a special bond: of militancy, friendship and mutual knowledge. Such links crossed borders, allowed confidential relationships to be nurtured and were fundamental for knowing the most secret decisions taken by the Soviet state.

The IUS was also a formidable propaganda vehicle for the youth of Africa and Latin America, allowing them to shape and influence the future ruling classes of many countries, prioritising decolonisation and support for oppressed peoples as their main objectives. Jacques Vergès (who represented the island of Réunion and headed the Committee of Anti-Colonial Students in Paris) worked exactly in the same vein, following Šelepin's guidance.

Paris and the activities of the Soviet secret services

Right after the end of the Bolshevik revolution Paris became the destination of a flood of Soviet emigrants, and the beating heart of a massive espionage operation. Agents despatched by Moscow would abduct and kill exiled members of the White Movement. Such actions were not only assisted, but actually backed by the French Communist Party. There is copious evidence for many infamous cases of the PCF cooperating with the NKVD and the KGB. From 1929 and following Paul Muraille's lead, Soviet intelligence started employing so-called "people's correspondents" (or *rabkors*, for *rabochy korrespondent*), who were officially supposed to report to the newspaper *L'Humanité* on the social conflicts raging within French factories. In fact, the people's correspondents were carrying information that would eventually reach the Red Army. Among their number were Claude Liogier, Izaiah Bir and Jacques Duclos, who would later become the party's number two. He was working for the Komintern and one of its most important bases was the celebrated Hôtel D'Alsace, where Oscar Wilde died in November 1900. In 1932 the underground network's actions were curtailed following several arrests, and it was only after the Second World War that the PCF resumed its role in critical espionage cases. While military and industrial espionage were its core activities, several NKVD operations aiming to exterminate Stalin's opponents were also carried out: the abduction of the White Guard General Miller; the killing of the banker Dmitry Navashin; the suspected murder of Leon Trotsky's son in 1937; and that of the rebel agent Ignatz Reiss. During the Second World War efforts had been made to infiltrate several Soviet spies into General De Gaulle's entourage. They would find themselves in an extremely privileged position after the war. Among them was a prominent character in many a shady post-war plot; a man who later, in 1944, appointed by De Gaulle himself, would become the Minister of the Interior in the French interim government: Emmanuel d'Astier de La Vigerie. Around the same time another French secret agent was recruited who would be unmasked only in 1963: George Pâques. In the early post-war era French intelligence, which had its name changed from DGER (*Direction Générale de l'Enseignement et de la Recherche*) to SDECE (External Documentation and Counter-Espionage Service) in November 1944, was in a sorry state. Colonel Passy, the head of the Gaullist espionage network in London since April 1945, fired most of the staff, which had already been penetrated by too many enemy agents and PCF militants. This shake-up, passionately attacked by the PCF even in the pages of *L'Humanité*, weakened and crippled the organisation, making it even more vulnerable to infiltration by undercover KGB and GRU agents. One typical example was that of Sandor Rado, a Soviet agent in Geneva during the war, who got into France in the summer of 1944 bearing a fake identity. A KGB agent who defected to the West in the 1960s claimed that there was a Soviet agent who had set up home in south-eastern France when the war ended. The local PCF helped him get new papers, and he settled down so well that he even became the mayor of the town he lived in.

When the Allies liberated Paris, the PCF had a striking quantitative edge in terms of the police: in 1945, 3,000 out of 22,000 Parisian police agents were also members of the PCF. It was thus the best of times for the Communist party to employ their police force to produce all the fake IDs it could. The post-war years were also a convenient time for people connected to the USSR to sneak into France's public and manufacturing sectors. Pierre Guay and Alexander Volodin—two infamous French collaborators during the Nazi occupation—had their shady past wiped clean by the PCF in return for their loyalty to the party. They too were provided with fake papers that erased any trace of their responsibilities during the war; moreover, a DGER official and PCF member helped them through the whole process and even got Volodin into French intelligence.

Both Volodin and Guay enjoyed a glittering career at the pinnacle of the Gaullist establishment. They spent years close to Soviet agents in France and played key roles in several ministries. Although they had been revealed as former collaborators, they were virtually untouchable (the accusations against them were barred by statute) and, surprisingly enough, they were never condemned for their crimes.

De Gaulle and Soviet infiltration in France

In the spring of 1962, General De Gaulle received a confidential letter from US President John Kennedy, delivered by a special emissary, who handed it to the French president in person. It was a warning, based on intelligence provided by an informer now in the US, about Soviet infiltration of French intelligence. What was worse, the agents were even present in De Gaulle's own office. No safe means of communication were open to De Gaulle, so he secretly sent General De Rougemont to Washington, so that he could force out a first-hand confession from the informer. The interrogation lasted for three days, at the end of which De Rougemont had no doubts: the threat was real, and it was everywhere. The mole who was coming clean with the Americans was Anatoliy Golitsyn; formerly a major in the KGB, who had defected to the CIA in December 1961 while he was in Helsinki. He was now providing the USA with massive amounts of precious information. It looked like an amazing intelligence windfall for the Americans, but something stood in their way: Golitsyn didn't know the names of the infiltrators he was revealing. He could only inform on what they did and where they did it. Nonetheless, his reports led to the arrest of several Soviet moles: one of them was Georges Pâques, who was working for NATO and was caught red-handed and arrested in August 1963 for revealing classified information to the enemy. With Pâques, however—as well as with several disloyal agents—the French government was curiously lenient. The first verdict Pâques was given in 1964 was life imprisonment for high treason; the sentence, though, was commuted into twenty years of imprisonment, and in the end he was pardoned by President Pompidou in 1970. One of Michel Debré's technical counsellors in the early '60s, Constantin Melnik, confirmed that the Gaullist party was swarming with KGB agents that were never caught. According to Golitsyn, nested in the bosom of the SDECE was a KGB network that went by the name of "Saphir", in which a dozen agents operated. Golitsyn also knew about the overhaul the SDECE had gone through, and he could also recall the names of several agents. Now that such a large network of moles had come to light, it was easier to understand why so many secret operations had fallen through in previous years. The most infamous, as well as the most important one, had been the so-called "Minos operation", financed by the CIA and backed by the SDECE. The French army had trained up several anti-communist fugitives from Czechoslovakia, then airdropped them into Slovakia hoping to muster up an armed resistance movement. But the Czechoslovakian intelligence services had been warned about the plan: a platoon of soldiers was waiting for the disloyal paratroopers, who were probably executed for high treason. After the failure of the Minos operation, the CIA changed their mind about the French intelligence services and began treating them with great circumspection.

Golitsyn also reported that a former minister very close to De Gaulle, as well as several other French statesmen, were on the Soviet payroll. The person Golitsyn was referring to had been amid De Gaulle's *coterie* during the war and had even been a minister in the General's interim government. There were a few possible suspects, and among them was Louis Joxe, though no evidence was ever found against him. Joxe had been a secretary in the interim government from 1945 to 1946, and an ambassador in Moscow from 1952 to 1953. Another highly suspected person—and quite unsettlingly, for his personal details matched Golitsyn's indications—was no less than Emmanuel d'Astier de La Vigerie, the minister of the interior in De Gaulle's interim government in 1944. D'Astier de La Vigerie had also been the editor of *Libération*, the newspaper financed by the PCF, right until its closure in 1964 (the PCF newspaper had no relation whatsoever with the modern newspaper of the same name: *Libération*). Even though he had been on the hard right before the war, during the Resistance he jumped on the PCF's bandwagon. It was thanks to the communists' votes that he later obtained his parliamentary seat. At the suggestion of Louis Aragon, he was awarded the Lenin Prize in 1957 for his "efforts in maintaining the peace". He was a frequent visitor to the USSR and married a Russian woman, the daughter of the former ambassador, Leonid Krasin. According to General Krivitsky—one of the most important Soviet agents, who fled to the West and was murdered in a Washington hotel in 1940—the PCF's shadow party, the left-wing *Union progressiste*, was actually founded by d'Astier de La Vigerie and Pierre Cot, another man close to Moscow. D'Astier de La Vigerie reached the pinnacles of the World Peace Council, which had been established by the Cominform, and was a regular at the Russian embassy. In his memoirs of his seven-year-long term as President of France, Vincent Auriol noted: "There is almost no-one I loathe as much as d'Astier de La Vigerie. He is nothing but a mere pawn in the PCF's hands. He is always satisfied and he would allow everything. There must be a skeleton in his cupboard. What was his crime, that he feels he is bound to pay off like this?" D'Astier had written several racist and anti-Semitic pamphlets in the Thirties; then, during the war, he suddenly aligned with De Gaulle and then with the Communist party. He would talk of himself as a "very left-wing Gaullist", and both De Gaulle and the Soviets held him in high regard. In 1948 he took issue with Camus in *Libération*, attacking him for his pacifism. "You are a pacifist, and yet your social movement for peace is like an anti-tuberculosis movement that aims at holding back the sick rather than preventing contagion". According to Olivier Todd, Camus regarded d'Astier as a double-crosser and an unprincipled Stalinist.

Their dispute continued on the pages of *L'action* and in the bimonthly newspaper *La gauche*, and at its core there was the debate about Marxism and how to overcome capitalism.

Such words were slaps in the face of those who sought to present the French people with a rosy picture of

Stalinist society. Their real target—their enemy no. 1—was now Camus.

At that time, Service Action, the executive branch of SDECE dedicated to assassinations, was operating at the highest level to eliminate members of the Algerian subversion in Europe. According to Prime Minister Debré's Security Adviser, Constantin Melnik, Service Action murdered 135 people in 1960, and in 1961, 103. The coincidence of interests ahead of Khrushchev's visit may have allowed the unspeakable: a collaboration of Service Action to the operation of the KGB. In fact, as Constantin Melnik reports, the tyre tampering technique was used by Service Action in the attempt on the life of arms dealer Otto Schlüter: a micro explosive charge applied to the wheel of his Porsche had crushed the tyre when the car had exceeded 120 kilometers per hour (140 according to another version: the same presumed speed of the car in which Camus lost his life, due to the blowout of the tyre).

Camus and Khrushchev's trip to Paris

The memoirs of Oleg Kalugin—a KGB general who fled to the West after thirty years of service for the USSR—published in the US in 1994, is replete with unsettling comments about the French intelligence services, which were allegedly more heavily infiltrated by Soviet agents than any other Western country. Kalugin wrote:

> In 1973, before I joined the counter-intelligence, I already knew that there were numerous infiltrators of ours in France. Even so, the number of high-rank moles on our

payroll amidst the French army, intelligence and counter-intelligence amazed me. Back then there were a dozen excellent agents working for us in France, and each was a leader of their sector. We had our hands all over the French intelligence, which all the more appeared to us terribly leaky and flawed.

Such levels of infiltration could achieve more than attain a shared objective, such as Camus' assassination: it could also work as an independent service, going largely unnoticed by the uncorrupted part of the French espionage establishment. Jacques Vergès' hints at a tacit agreement between the French and the Soviet intelligence about Camus' death is especially disturbing. In 1960, the same year as Camus' death, an operation led by Khrushchev was carried out in order to bring Maurice Dejean, the French ambassador in Moscow from 1955 to 1964, over to the USSR's side. Khrushchev said that "France is the crucial link in the chain that will bring Europe into our hands, and we must get hold of it". In October 1959, De Gaulle formally invited Khrushchev to spend a few months in Paris. It is little wonder that Albert Camus' reaction to the USSR leader and his foreign politics was not exactly of the friendliest kind. France and the USSR were getting closer and closer and Camus stood in the way, casting an admonishing, baneful shadow on both countries. It might have been then that the decision was taken that Camus was inconvenient; he was too popular and too charismatic and might jeopardise the increasingly close French-Soviet affiliation. In late March 1960 Khrushchev went on a week-long tour through France and was warmly welcomed by the PCF all over the country. What of Camus, though, the powers that be wondered? What if he publicly blamed the illustrious visitor for the gory occupation of Hungary—for the bloody suppression of his opponents; or for the Gulag? Neither of the diplomatic services involved would allow such a hostile reaction: Khrushchev was only to be praised and welcomed as befitted the leader of a prestigious allied power. Sergei Vinogradov, the USSR ambassador in Paris, a genial man and a *bon vivant*, was held in the highest regard by French politicians and the Parisian middle-class, and he never missed a public event or a celebration. A long-time good acquaintance of De Gaulle's, he was a regular at Colombey-les-Deux-Églises (De Gaulle's personal retreat) before the general returned to power. France and the USSR had never been closer: six years later, misled by his not-too-unconcerned counsellors, De Gaulle would decide to take France out of NATO.

Khrushchev's visit to France in late March and early April 1960 was momentous, a milestone on the path of cooperation between Paris and Moscow—a goal to be achieved at all costs. Camus died on 4 January the same year, in broad daylight, on the large, straight, nearly empty road that led to Paris. Khrushchev's plane would land at Orly on 23 March. No discordant voice would be left to spoil the sumptuous, meek, welcoming chorus.

The Trémeaud crime and the Czech secret services in Paris

In October 1956, France's major focus of public debate was the integration of West Germany into the European

Economic Community (EEC), which occurred in 1957. It was then that anonymous letters from a self-proclaimed armed group campaigning for Germany's independence were sent to hundreds of prominent people in Eastern France (the regions of the Bas-Rhin and the Haut-Rhin). All the letters bore a swastika, and referred to the recipients of the letters as "French oppressors" and stated their anger at the French occupation of Alsace-Lorraine. Threats were made against all French people willing to force their rotten, corrupt culture upon the occupied. An especially harsh punishment would be inflicted upon French "spies, agents and teachers" for their crimes. The French police were absolutely oblivious to the existence of such an armed group, so their investigation was sloppy and they concluded that this particular *Kampfverband* or hit team was nothing more than a petty neo-Nazi group from Hamburg. On 14 May 1957, Prefect André-Marie Trémeaud invited several senior figures to his home in Strasbourg for the closing ceremony of an ECSC session. That morning the prefect had received a box of Cuban cigars, allegedly sent from Havana's salesperson in Europe. Trémeaud's secretary brought him the cigars and he put them away, intending to offer them to his guests at that night's party. However, the cigar box was forgotten and no-one touched it till 17 May when the prefect handed the box to his wife so she could offer cigars to their guests. Madame Henriette Trémeaud went upstairs and asked her maid for a tray on which to arrange the cigars, then opened the box. A deafening explosion tore the room apart and Trémeaud's wife died on the spot. Further police investigation revealed that the address of the sender on the cigar box had been typed with the same typewriter used in the *Kampfverband*'s letters. The French press had a field-day, reporting on a potential comeback of Nazi extremism in Germany. Further enquiries, however, drew a blank: the dubious neo-Nazi group seemed to be undetectable.

In 1968, Ladislav Bittman, an agent of the Czech intelligence service, or State Security (StB) who specialised in misinformation, defected to the West and finally shed light on the Trémeaud case. The whole operation aimed at undermining the relationship between France and Germany had been arranged by the KGB in Moscow. The StB had then been entrusted with carrying it out. After the anonymous neo-Nazi letters were sent out, four agents from Czech intelligence were dispatched to Paris: Miloslav Kouba, Robert Ther, Milan Kopecky and Stanislas Tomes. It was they who had sent the parcel bomb to Trémeaud from a post office in Boulevard Diderot: their ultimate goal was to torpedo the European Economic Union and the European Single Market, which was to come into effect on 1 January 1958. The mastermind of the plan was KGB General Ivan Agayants: he would pursue his objective of destabilising Europe and defaming West Germany up until the Sixties, fanning the fears of neo-Nazism and arranging the desecration of synagogues, Jewish cemeteries and monuments to Jews both in Europe and worldwide. The campaign of desecration started in Cologne on 25 December 1959 and continued in Antwerp, Copenhagen, London, Glasgow, Milan, Paris, Oslo, Stockholm and Vienna. On 3 January

1960, targets were hit in Athens, Manchester, Melbourne and Perth, and on 6 January there were desecrations as far afield as Buenos Aires and Bogotá. It was the peak of activity for the KGB and the StB; France and Germany were the sitting targets of both intelligence agencies destabilisation plans.

Albert Camus was the next to fall, on a large, straight, empty road a few miles from Paris, on 4 January 1960.